Female Offenders

Female Offenders
Correctional Afterthoughts

by
Robert R. Ross
and
Elizabeth A. Fabiano

McFarland & Company, Inc., Publishers
Jefferson, North Carolina, and London

Robert R. Ross, Ph.D., is currently professor of criminology, University of Ottawa. His experience includes more than twenty years as a psychologist in Canadian prisons, twelve as chief psychologist with the Ontario Ministry of Correctional Services. He was awarded the Centennial Medal of Canada "for contribution to the nation in the field of delinquency." His books include *Self-Mutilation, Effective Correctional Treatment, Prison Guard/Correctional Officer, Treatment of the Alcohol-Abusing Offender,* and *Time to Think: A Cognitive Model of Crime and Delinquency Prevention and Rehabilitation* (with Elizabeth A. Fabiano).

Elizabeth A. Fabiano, a professional criminologist, has an M.A. from the University of Ottawa. She has worked with juvenile and adult offenders, as a researcher in sociology, as a teacher of learning-disabled children, and as project worker for the Ontario Ministry of Education. She has co-authored many monographs in the areas of cognitive assessment, cognitive intervention, and correctional services, including *Time to Think: A Cognitive Model of Crime and Delinquency Prevention and Rehabilitation* (with Robert R. Ross).

Library of Congress Catalog Card Number 85-43588

ISBN 0-89950-217-2 (sewn softcover; acid-free natural paper) 

Printed in the United States of America

McFarland Box 611 Jefferson NC 28640

Acknowledgments

The research reported in this book was prepared for and supported by the Research Division, Secretariat, Ministry of the Solicitor General of Canada. It is based on an earlier report which was prepared for and supported by the Planning and Research Branch, Ontario Ministry of Correctional Services: *The Female Offender: Treatment and Training* (R.R. Ross, C. Currie & B. Krug-McKay, 1980). The present report provides an update and revision of the earlier report. It also extends the earlier report by including a discussion of research on systems intervention and by presenting a model (the social competence model) for guiding intervention initiatives.

We are grateful to Andy Birkenmayer who stimulated and encouraged the research for the original report. We appreciate the contribution of Claudia Currie and Barbara Krug-McKay who served as researchers for the original study.

We are grateful to Dr. Bob Cormier and Dr. Frank Porporino who suggested and supported the research for the revised report.

The views expressed in this book are those of the authors and do not necessarily reflect the views of the Ontario Ministry of Correctional Services or the Ministry of the Solicitor General of Canada.

We gratefully acknowledge the assistance of B. D. Ross, R. D. Ross and Ronald Clément in compiling the indexes and proofreading.

Contents

Introduction

Politicians, criminal justice policy-makers and correctional managers have come under increasing pressure to improve the quantity, variety and availability of programs for female offenders. The pressure stems largely from a number of interrelated factors:

- There has been a significant increase in the number of arrests of female offenders and a substantial increase in the number of females entering the correctional system (Adams, 1978; Chesney-Lind, 1978; Simon, 1975).
- Individuals and groups concerned with women's issues have brought considerable attention to the treatment of females in the criminal justice system.
- Allegations that women are unfairly discriminated against in the criminal justice system have led to demands (and sometimes court orders) for equal opportunities for women in correctional facilities, services and program opportunities (Arditi, Goldberg, Hartle, Peters & Phelps, 1973; Berzins & Cooper, 1982; Singer, 1973).
- A small but important increase in women's participation in correctional management, in academic programs in criminology, and in organizations in the private sector which are concerned with criminal justice, has greatly increased interest in and concern for women in the correctional system (Nicolai, 1981).

Equity or Quality?

> *The only apparent advantage women have over men in America's penal system is that fewer of them are exposed to it.*
>
> (Burkhart, 1973)

Most of the pressure seems to be directed toward ensuring women equality in program opportunities. Too often the demand has been simply that female offenders should be provided with the same services and programs that are presently available for male offenders. Too often the proponents of equality have given little consideration to the possibility that the services and programs (the ones provided for males) may be of little benefit for females (or males!). The assumption seems to be: "If it is given to males it should be given to females." Seldom considered is the possibility that some of the programs being sought for women should not be given to anyone.

The establishment of "equal rights" is undeniably important, but its achievement may not be sufficient to ensure an adequate correctional response to the needs of female offenders. Equality may engender a state of affairs in which female offenders will be able to obtain only programs which are designed for male offenders rather than programs which are designed for and needed by women. As Brodsky (1974) has noted, "The possibility is that the special problems of women will continue to wait until general reforms for men have been implemented."

Effective policy formation, program planning and development for female offenders requires more than an equal rights rationale. Also required is a demand for quality programs, for effective programs, and for programs and services which have value. That requires careful assessment of the characteristics of female offenders, their needs, problems and strengths, and thorough assessment of the relevance and value of current correctional programs and services for women. It also requires a careful examination and articulation of the principles and goals which programs and services should operationalize as well as a determination of the kinds of practices which have the greatest probability of achieving these goals. It requires careful planning based on a rational strategy. It may be found that what is required is the provision not only of programs which have been provided for males, but also of programs which have not been provided for anyone.

Too often corrections has responded to pressure and criticism by initiatives that represent what is "in vogue" rather than what is needed. Consequently, program development occurs in a piecemeal or even haphazard manner. Correctional services for female offenders epitomize that phenomenon.

This book is designed to yield some basic information which might contribute to the development of a rational policy for female offenders. It presents the results of a critical review of the literature on correctional intervention programs for female offenders in community and institutional settings. The review was designed to:

- Determine the nature and variety of programs which have been provided in North America for female offenders in institutional and community settings.
- Determine the extent to which such programs have been evaluated and assess the quality of these evaluations.
- Identify programs which have been demonstrated to be effective, or appear to have particular promise for reducing recidivism or for ameliorating behavioral problems in female offenders.
- By comparing effective and ineffective programs, identify the components of programs which appear to be associated with success.
- Ascertain the degree to which programs for female offenders incorporate the principles and practices which research has found to be associated with effective correctional programming.
- Identify critical issues in program conceptualization, offender classification and service delivery.

The primary objective of the review was to identify those programs which research has found to be effective, and to determine which program models and practices appear to be the best investment for an increasing population of female offenders.

The review was based on a search of the published literature on programs for juvenile and adult female offenders identified by a computerized bibliographic retrieval search provided by the Solicitor General's library (June, 1984), an earlier review (Ross, Currie & Krug-McKay, 1980), and an examination of recent literature on the characteristics and needs of female offenders. Since the vast majority of information on the treatment of female offenders is buried within reports on the treatment of male offenders and cannot be identified through standard bibliographic retrieval procedures, an additional examination was made of recent literature on the treatment of offenders in general; programs which specifically mentioned that female subjects were included in the study were examined.

The results of the review are presented in the following chapters. Chapter 1 describes some findings with respect to the general status of correctional programming for females, and identifies several social/political factors which have influenced the development of correctional services for females. Chapter 2 discusses the effectiveness of a variety of programs which have been provided: psychotherapy, behavior modification, therapeutic communities, alcohol and drug abuse programs, family therapy, education, vocational training, life skills programs, social skills training, cognitive training and moral development programs. Chapter 3 discusses a number of correctional services: probation, parole, community residential services, work release, health care, child-care, co-corrections and classification. Chapter 4 discusses the implications of the review for policy formation, program development and research.

1. General Observations and Issues

One very clear impression is conveyed by this literature: In general, treatment and training programs for female offenders are distinctively poorer in quantity, quality, and variety, and considerably different in nature from those for male offenders. A large number of reports suggest that correctional programs have typically been conceived by males for males and only later, often as an afterthought, extended to female offenders, for whom they may be thoroughly inappropriate (Adler, 1975; Adler & Simon, 1979; Bowker, 1978; Contact, 1978; Crites, 1976; Gibson, 1973; Glick & Neto, 1977; Milton, Pierce, Lyons & Furry, 1976; Simon, 1975; Singer, 1973; Skoler & McKeown, 1974; Smart, 1976).

Although correctional management in *some* jurisdictions have provided *some* kinds of services more frequently to females than to males, the preponderance of evidence supports the conclusion that, in general, female offenders have received far less than an equitable share of program opportunities. For example, a national study of the range of programs available to female offenders in jails, prisons and community settings in fourteen states in the U.S. resulted in the following conclusions:

> Treatment in correctional institutions was conspicuous by its absence. Treatment staff ... were most often involved in intake testing, court ordered examinations, and ... prescribing medication. Counseling was often a duty of correctional officers who were not necessarily trained and whose primary role was custodial ... tranquilizers may be used instead of program[s] to help maintain control in an institutional setting ... in many jails religion was the only program offered.
>
> (Glick & Neto, 1977)

A recent task force on women reported that, in the U.S., "only five percent of all federally funded juvenile delinquency projects were specifically female-related and only six per cent of all local monies for juvenile justice were spent on programs for females" (Milton, Pierce, Lyons & Hippensteel, 1977). It has also been reported that female offenders are often held in detention not because they present a threat to society, but because of a lack of alternative facilities, services, and programs. In New York, "rehabilitation programs for women offenders serve about 25 out of every 1,000 offenders" (Bradshaw & Ecks, 1977).

In Canada,

> ... they have been given the left-overs and hand-me-downs of facilities and programs designed for men; and when nothing has been left over to hand down, a poor imitation of the model, an outmoded version, has been hastily provided, with inferior facilities, less space, fewer programs and at less cost.
>
> (Berzins & Cooper, 1982)

It must be emphasized that such major national surveys tend to foster erroneous impressions and gross overgeneralizations about the status of treatment for women offenders because they aggregate the information across facilities, locations, and jurisdictions. They fail to give attention to those settings in which exceptional service is provided. The availability and quality of services vary greatly depending on the jurisdiction (e.g. federal vs. state/provincial); the setting (community vs. institution); the facility (jail vs. prison); the location (rural vs. urban); the accessibility to community services; and the particular type of program (e.g., psychiatric treatment vs. vocational training).

Corrections in Context

A number of social, political, financial, administrative, and ideological factors appear to have influenced the development (or the neglect) of programs for female offenders.

• **Numerical reality:** Even with recent increases in crimes committed by females (e.g. Adams, 1978; Chesney-Lind, 1978; Simon, 1975), the number of female offenders entering the correctional system is extremely low in comparison with that of males, whose greater number has commanded greater attention.

• **Costs:** Because female offenders comprise just four to seven percent of the offender population, less than extravagant correctional agency budgets allow only meager resources for female offenders.

> Women represent more than half of the total population of Canada. Their remarkable underrepresentation in the criminal population is saving the taxpayers millions of dollars annually. This consideration in itself should render obsolete any attempt to curtail services to convicted women on the basis of higher per capita costs per imprisoned offender.
>
> (Berzins and Cooper, 1982)

It is usually thought that services can be delivered much more efficiently (in terms of the number of clients treated) by spending available monies in male facilities, which tend to be much more densely populated. However it is ironic that

> ... when innovation is suggested for men's institutions, the objective is raised: It's too big; when innovation is suggested for women's institutions ... it's too small!
>
> (Gibson, 1973)

• **Time:** Sentences for many female offenders are thought to be too short to enable them to profit from educational, vocational, or therapeutic programs.

• **Classification:** Classification, which is a cornerstone of correctional programming for male offenders, is frequently nonexistent for female offenders, whose small numbers, it is reasoned, make it prohibitive to provide separate facilities or services appropriate to their needs (even their security needs). Ironically, it is the existence of classification (by sex) which has resulted in the limited program opportunities available to female offenders by isolating them from the general population and, thus, from facilities and services.

• **Double-standard justice:** It has been argued that the criminal justice system responds to female criminality in terms of its presumed sexual aspects, perpetuates a Victorian view of female sexuality, and responds protectively and paternalistically to the female offender, particularly in the case of juveniles (Haft, 1974; Morton, 1976). This frame of reference has led to the view that custody itself provides all the treatment necessary since it removes the offender from the "unregulated sexual marketplace ... and forces them to save their sexual favours, moral reputations, and health until they are of marriageable age" (Schlossman & Wallach, 1978, p.76).

• **Less violent crimes:** Because their crimes are less likely to be of a violent nature, female offenders are seldom seen as dangerous or as constituting a serious threat to the social order (Haft, 1974; Miller, 1977; Goodman, Maloney & Davis, 1976). Since they present little threat, it is often believed they need little treatment.

• **Riots:** Although disturbances which might draw attention to their treatment are not foreign to institutions for female offenders, they appear to be less frequent, less dramatic, and less publicized than those in male institutions (Crites, 1976; Gibson, 1973; Simon, 1975). Moreover, prisons for women often *look* more serene. Accordingly, less attention has been drawn to conditions in women's prisons. Much of the literature on prisons for females suggests that female offenders are more likely to accept their lot in prison, and are less likely to grieve their conditions, particularly by means of lawsuit. (This, in part, is because they have less access to law libraries.) It has been suggested that they tend to express their hostility inward, against themselves, rather than against their environment. They have been described as "insignificant irritants to the smooth running of law and order" (Smart, 1976, p. 2).

• **Nonpersons:** Female offenders "are twofold deviants: not only have they deviated from the general male standards of conduct by reason of being female, but they have deviated from male standards of female conduct by being offenders" (Adler, 1975, p. 173). Accordingly, in the eyes of the public and the criminal justice system they have often been relegated to the status of nonpersons, undeserving of special attention.

• **Poor prognosis:** Because, it is argued, the criminal justice system tends to be chivalrous and lenient towards most women who break the law, those who enter the correctional system are often thought to be the very worst and to have little potential for change (Singer, 1973). Accordingly, it is considered that there is little point in wasting valuable resources on them. (One might think that it would be judged that they are the offenders most in need of services!)

• **"Hysteria":**

> ...because doctors and psychiatrists "know" that women complain more about less serious symptoms they will counterbalance this effect by giving them less serious attention.
>
> (Smart, 1976, p. 162)

• **Faith in Chivalry:** Until recently, because of traditional social expectations about the treatment of women, it seems to have been *assumed* that, because they are women, female offenders would be treated in a benign and gentle way in the correctional setting. As a result, there has been less pressure to determine how they *actually* have been treated.

Correctional Sexism

The criminal justice system, a behemoth dominated by men and male ways of looking at the world, represents the most formal development of cross-sex controls in human society.
(Bowker, 1978, p. XIII)

Ideological factors have not only had a major influence on the availability of programs for female offenders, they have also determined their nature. By far the majority of program efforts have been directed to training female offenders in traditional feminine pursuits. It has been argued that most correctional services for females have been designed by males and reflect the stereotypical traditional sex role of women in our culture (e.g. Feinman, 1979; Smart, 1976; Bowker, 1978). Since women have not been seen as breadwinners, there has been little impetus for providing them with training in meaningful and marketable employment skills. In keeping with their traditional roles they are more likely to have been provided with "busy-work" or "women's work."

The implicit syllogism determining the nature of program services for female offenders seems to have been:

A. Criminal women have deviated from traditional female sex roles;

B. Traditional females are noncriminal;

C. Therefore, criminal women need training in those skills which allow them to assume their traditional and "proper" role.

The view of female offenders as actual or potential mothers and housekeepers has led to a concentration of services on training them for this role. According to some correctional administrators, the fact that a girl is delinquent proves that she has not learned to revere domestic pursuits and needs to do so.

> Instruction in domesticity was allied with the reformatory's marital goals: inmates would become so devoted to and skilled at domestic chores that they would easily attract husbands. It was as if ... a rigorous pursuit of domesticity would compensate for the girls' previous immorality.
>
> (Schlossman & Wallach, 1978, p. 77)

Therapy vs. Training

It has been assumed that women are more likely to experience distress while incarcerated and, therefore, are more in need of counselling services (Gibson, 1976; Smart, 1976). Unfortunately, this view has led to excessive focus on the offender's emotional adjustment and a relative lack of concern with her interpersonal or vocational skills. Until very recently, female crime was usually "explained" as the result of anatomical, physiological, or psychological aberrations, abnormalities, or deficiencies in the individual (Klein, 1973). The assumption that they are likely to evidence biological deficiencies or psychopathology has led to the view that they have greater needs for treatment. In keeping with such causal assumptions, treatment typically has taken the form of psychodynamic psychotherapy.

Women and Madness

It has been convincingly argued that there is a sexist bias in psychiatric diagnosis both in the mental health system and in criminal justice (Smart, 1976). The assumption that women in general are more vunerable to mental illness and emotional disturbance has led to the notion that females in the criminal justice system require more treatment services of a medical/psychiatric nature—particularly drugs. Sometimes, it has also led to "longer or indeterminate sentences so that they have time to benefit from treatment" (Haft, 1974).

It has also been assumed that because of differential arrest, conviction, and sentencing practices, adjudicated female offenders, particularly those who are incarcerated, represent a select group of offenders with a higher than normal incidence of deficiencies and abnormalities and, therefore, a higher need for therapy (Crites, 1976).

There has been a tendency to assume that female offenders are more likely to be passive, compliant and dependent and, therefore, more willing to accept a relationship with a therapist (Gibson, 1973; Smart, 1976). Unfortunately, this view has led to an inordinate use of therapies which aim to engender client improvement through attempts to establish close personal relationships with the offenders rather than through training them in social or vocational skills.

Clients or Subjects?

Although women have been provided with fewer programs and services than men, there are some considerations which might lead one to expect they should receive *more* services than their male counterparts. Thus, it has been argued that because recidivism rates for female offenders are often much lower than for males (e.g., Gibson, 1976), women are more likely to benefit from rehabilitative programs than are men. It has also been argued that because female offenders are fewer in number and are housed in smaller units, programs for them, including innovative ones, could be more easily implemented, managed and evaluated (Crites, 1976). In fact, the rehabilitation model in corrections was pioneered by institutions for women, and many services were innovated in women's prisons, which have been labelled "laboratories for prison reform" (Gibson, 1976). However, it is a moot point whether such innovative services were designed for the benefit of the women or whether they were merely guinea pigs for the study of programs which could later be provided for the larger population of male offenders. Ironically, many of the programs which were pioneered for women are no longer available to them (Gibson, 1976).

Literature

The term "forgotten offender" has frequently been used to indicate the fact that in the criminological literature, female offenders have been systematically ignored. In books and journals until the mid '70s, female offenders were often only footnotes. Since the publication of Freda Adler's *Sisters in Crime* in 1975, the literature has greatly expanded. Countless journal articles and at least twelve books on women and crime have appeared in the past eight years alone. Most of the recent literature has been concerned with issues such as increasing crime rates among females, the impact of the women's movement, and discrimination against women in the criminal justice system.

With some notable exceptions (e.g. Chapman, 1980; Glick & Neto, 1977), correctional programs and services are discussed, if at all, only as further evidence of sexism in criminal justice. There have been very few systematic studies of the effectiveness of programs for females.

Policy Development

There is very little evidence that policy or program development has been based on examination of program efficacy or on systematic investigation of the female offender's needs. Program development in recent years appears to have been responsive almost exclusively to views about the needs of women in general, without adequate consideration of the particular needs or interests of female *offenders*, which may, or may not, be the same as those of women in the larger population. Policy seems to have been based on sentiment, conjecture, fads, and politics. With the exception of the much-maligned medical model, there appears to be no rational model of the needs of female offenders which has guided policy and program development. Until recently, apart from the medical model, the only "model" that seems to have influenced the development of programs for females is the "male model":

> ...their needs have never been documented. Their facilities and programs have not been designed for them. It has been assumed that a smaller-scale version of what was available for men would suit them, and, when that smaller version proved to be uneconomical, even that was no longer considered.
>
> (Berzins & Cooper, 1982, p.405)

The major current models are the "equity model" or the "forget-me-not model." Actually, they are exhortations or pleas rather than models. It remains to be seen whether they lead to programs which actually fit the needs of female offenders or whether they only entrench the "male model" more solidly.

2. Programs

In this chapter we present a state-of-the-art review of a number of program modalities which have been used with female offenders or with mixed groups of male and female offenders.

Individual Psychotherapy

Undoubtedly, the most popular treatment programs for female offenders, both adolescent and adult, have been the psychotherapies. The popularity of these programs probably reflects the widespread view that criminality in females is an indication of some underlying psychopathological condition. Their popularity does not attest to the efficacy of such programs. The outcome of research raises major doubts about the adequacy of the disease model of female criminality.

Studies of the value of individual psychotherapy with offenders have been almost entirely limited to individual case studies, which seldom provide anything more than anecdotal evidence of success or failure. In most cases, only testimonials from the therapists are provided. Moreover, such studies usually describe programs for atypical clients. There is no convincing evidence of the value of individual psychodynamic psychotherapy either for reducing the emotional or behavioral problems of female offenders or reducing their posttreatment criminal behavior. In making this statement, we hasten to remind the reader that in the case of individual psychotherapy, as in the case of every other intervention we discuss, the lack of evidence of the effectiveness of these programs does *not* indicate that they have no value, but only that whatever value they may have has not been demonstrated in methodologically adequate research.

Group Psychotherapy

Group psychotherapy and group counselling have been much more extensively researched. However, the quality of the research has been poor, and program outcome has been mixed. Several studies have found that group therapy failed to yield improvements on personality measures (e.g. Bailey, 1970; Mandel & Vinnes, 1968; Rothenberg, 1969). When improvement on personality tests has been found, it is usually the case that this improvement has not generalized to reconviction rates (e.g. Taylor, 1967). Several studies have found that group therapy had no significant effect on either the institutional or community adjustment of either female delinquents (e.g. Adams, 1959; Sowles & Gill, 1970) or adult female offenders (Ketterling, 1970). Studies in which group therapy has been combined with individual psychotherapy have fared no better in terms of reducing delinquent behavior (Meyer, Borgatta, & Jones, 1965). At least one program which employed group therapy with delinquent girls found that the participants had a *higher* recidivism rate than untreated controls (Lampkin & Taylor, 1973).

There are many reports of positive outcomes from group therapy with female offenders, but they are plagued with methodological shortcomings, including small sample sizes (Redfering, 1972; 1973), subjective measures (Coleman, 1974; Goldberg, 1974), and absence of control groups (Peirce, 1963). Many programs reported success in modifying attitudes, but failed to assess changes in illegal behavior (James, Oxborn & Oetling, 1967; Marvit, 1972; Varki, 1977).

The research on group therapy does not yield much confidence in the value of this approach with female offenders. However, it is important to note that the poor quality of the research precludes any firm conclusion. With few exceptions, it is not possible to ascertain whether the quality of the services provided in any instance was sufficient to justify an expectation that the program might work.

The available studies have employed a wide range of intervention approaches under the label "group therapy," and program reports have seldom articulated clearly what this therapy comprises. It is often just not possible to know what "group therapy" refers to. Moreover, the studies have involved a wide variety of offender types and settings. The training, skills, personal characteristics of the therapists, and their commitment and effort are probably equally varied.

Well-controlled studies have clearly indicated that the type of therapist, the type of offender and the type of therapy (its nature, quality and intensity) are crucial determinants of the success or failure of group therapy with female offenders (McCord, 1977; Truax, Wargo & Silber, 1966; Truax, Wargo & Volksdorf, 1970). These studies demonstrated that reductions in recidivism could be obtained through programs which employed conscientious and well-qualified counsellors. Overall, however, the outcome of group therapy is mixed. Some offenders appear to have been helped, some have been unaffected and, for some, involvement in intensive group discussions with antisocial peers may have reinforced their delinquent orientations (McCord, 1977).

The only reasonable conclusion that can be made about the effects of group therapy with female offenders is that sometimes it "works" and sometimes it "fails" and the difference depends in large measure on who gives therapy to whom. One might wonder whether the benefits of therapy are a function of "therapy" or simply reflect exposure to therapists who are models of prosocial skills (Truax, Wargo & Volksdorf, 1970; Ross & Fabiano, 1985).

Therapeutic Community

• **Institutional communities:** The available research enables no firm conclusions either for or against the value of therapeutic communities in institutions for female offenders. Typically, reports on therapeutic communities extol the virtues of inmate participation, open communication, and shared decision-making. Typically, they provide no adequate evidence of improvements in the participants' institutional or postinstitutional adjustment (e.g. Bohme, Buhe & Schlutoro, 1978; Suarez, Haddox & Mittman, 1972; Thompson, 1968). In fact, in many instances they even fail to establish that a therapeutic community has actually been established.

Many of the programs which have been described as therapeutic communities have only the label, with none of the substance, of a therapeutic community. The negative reports on the outcome of such programs for female (or male) offenders (Romig, 1978) cannot be taken to reflect the inadequacy of the intervention strategy. More likely, they reflect the inadequacy of its application. One can only speculate whether those "therapeutic communities" which have failed have been therapeutic communities at all. Therapeutic community principles are readily compromised by institutional realities.

One might wonder why therapeutic communities have been so popular in institutions for female offenders in view of the number of investigators (including Maxwell Jones) who have raised serious doubts about the value of therapeutic communities within correctional settings. Jones (1976) suggests that its applicability may be limited to certain groups within the prison population. Specifically, he suggests that therapeutic communities will be most effective when implemented with first-time offenders exhibiting an above-average maturity level, residing in new institutions staffed by eager, willing, and trained staff. Inadequate training and poor motivation of the correctional staff (management and line staff) have often prevented a real therapeutic community from being established or maintained in correctional institutions (e.g. Suarez, et al., 1972).

The most extensive assessment of a therapeutic community for institutionalized female offenders is provided by research on the Vanier Centre for Women (Lambert & Madden, 1976). In a two year follow-up of 338 women, the recidivism rate was only 37 percent. However, in the absence of an adequate comparison or control group, it cannot be determined whether these results are better than no treatment at all.

The Vanier research did yield important information on three important aspects of therapeutic communities: program integrity, treatment by subject interaction, and postprogram variables. It confirmed Ochroch's (1957) findings that the success of therapeutic communities depends not only on the personal suitability, cooperation, enthusiasm, and application of the staff but also on the responsiveness of the institutional managers. In the Vanier study it was found that institutional adjustment and outcome depended on the particular cottage to which women were assigned. The most positive results were related to the degree to which the unit's program conformed to therapeutic community principles.

Finally, we should note that the goals of the program must be considered in assessing the value of therapeutic communities. Many have as their primary goal the reduction of inmate-staff and intra-inmate conflict (e.g. Suarez et al., 1972). Failure of such programs to exhibit reduced recidivism rates or success on other measures should not result in a condemnation of therapeutic communities.

•**"Drug-free" therapeutic communities:** A number of

residential, self-help, drug-free therapeutic communities for heroin and other drug addicts include female offender addicts. There is a dearth of adequate research on the efficacy of such programs not only with female offenders but also with male offenders. Research on the outcome of such programs does not enable a determination of the degree to which positive outcome is a function of the program or simply reflects the high motivation of those clients who satisfy the criteria for admission and continue in treatment (Glick & Neto, 1977).

Research on Synanon, the most touted of the "drug-free" communities has been thwarted by program directors. The research which is available fails to support the Synanon agents' strong claims of success (Markoff, 1966; Cherkas, 1965; Scott & Goldberg, 1973). The attrition rate is very high (as high as fifty percent, Scott & Goldberg, 1973) and of those who actually complete the program and leave, at least seventy-five percent relapse to drug use within two years (Switzer, 1974).

Research on Phoenix House in New York has demonstrated that this program results in decreased psychopathology and a reduction in depression, anger, anxiety, and suspiciousness (DeLeon, Skodol & Rosenthal, 1973). It has also been shown to reduce criminal behavior for those who complete the program as well as for those who remain only for three months (DeLeon, Holland & Rosenthal, 1972). However, it has not been adequately determined whether the success of the Phoenix House reflects the intervention or simply the motivation of its clients.

Many "drug-free" therapeutic communities include about twenty-five percent female addicts. No separate analysis has been made to determine the outcome for the females in those programs for which success has been claimed.

Odyssey House differs from many such communities by deliberately striving to ensure that clients are able and motivated to cope with living outside of the therapeutic community. Clients are helped to develop skills which will allow them to cope with the "outside" community and not just with the drug-free residence (Densen-Gerber & Drassner, 1974). Questions must be asked about the claims of "success" for clients who remain in the therapeutic community on a permanent basis; have they substituted a cult dependency for a chemical dependency?

Behavior Modification

There are no general statements which can be made about the efficacy of behavioral programs for female offenders. We acknowledge that there is clear evidence of the effectiveness of behavioral programs in modifying specific target behaviors such as acceptable behavior in academic classrooms (Meichenbaum, Bowers & Ross, 1968; Seymour & Sanson-Fisher, 1975); adherence to curfews (Alexander, 1976); emotional expressiveness (Ross & Palmer, 1976); prosocial conversational comments (Sanson-Fisher, Seymour & Baer, 1976; Sanson-Fisher, Seymour, Montgomery & Stokes, 1978); self-rewarding behavior (Thelen & Fryrear, 1971); work effort (Seymour & Stokes, 1976); and the elimination of nightmares (Ross, Meichenbaum & Humphrey, 1971). However, it has not been determined whether improvements in such behaviors have any bearing on delinquent or criminal behavior.

• **Institutional programs:** The success of behavioral programs depends very much on whether the program is conducted in an institutional setting or a community setting. As a means of reducing disciplinary infractions and improving participation and effort in academic or vocational programs, behavior modification appears to be useful at least with males (Braukman & Fixsen, 1975; Davidson & Seidman, 1974; Emory & Marholin, 1977; Ross & McKay, 1978). However, there is reason to doubt their value in improving the institutional behavior of female offenders. In one study with female adolescent offenders, a sophisticated token economy led to a five-fold *increase* in the incidence of self-mutilation, vandalism, escape attempts, and assault (Ross & McKay, 1978). The possibility that token economies may be an effective institutional management technique for male offenders, but not for females, needs to be studied by comparing the outcome of behavioral programs for females and males. Such studies have not been done.

There is no convincing evidence of the effectiveness of institutional token economies in terms of rehabilitation. Improving the institutional behaviors of female offenders may not generalize beyond the institution. In fact, the available evidence indicates that token economies in correctional institutions may increase recidivism (Ross & McKay, 1976; Ross & McKay, 1978).

Research indicates that the success of institutional behavioral programs depends on at least three major factors: 1. avoiding giving undue attention to negative antisocial behaviors, 2. focusing on improving the strength of prosocial behaviors and interpersonal skills, and 3. neutralizing the influence of the peer group mobilizing the peer group as a prosocial force.

The offender's peer group can pose a stumbling block for any correctional behavioral program. Typically, the peer group punishes prosocial behavior and reinforces antisocial behavior, thereby providing powerful opposition to the reward contingencies of the program director (Buehler, Patterson & Furniss, 1966; Duncan, 1972; Ross & McKay, 1976). By focusing behavioral programs on the extinction of antisocial behavior and doing so in a highly formalized manner (as in a token economy), program directors may only succeed in clearly articulating their authority and power and in providing explicit targets for the oppositional behavior of the adolescents. Giving female adolescents an important role in program development, motivating them to act as "therapists" for their peers (rather than as antisocial models), and training them in positive interpersonal skills which they can employ to help their peers has been demonstrated to be an effective way to improve both their institutional behavior (Sanson-Fisher, Seymour, Montgomery & Stokes, 1978) and their postinstitutional adjustment (Ross & McKay, 1976; Slack & Slack, 1976).

• **Community programs:** For the behavior modification enthusiast, much more encouraging results have been found in the outcome of community-based programs. Most of the correctional programs which have been demonstrated to be effective in methodologically adequate research are community correctional programs based on a behavioral/social learning model (Ross & Gendreau, 1980).

Several successful behavioral programs have been conducted in community residential settings. Thus, improvements in behavior in the residence have been reported for residences which have employed token economies (e.g. Marholin, Plienis, Harris, Marholin, 1975; Fixsen, Phillips & Wolf, 1973; Wagner & Breitmeyer, 1975). However, it must be noted that in each instance, the token economy comprised only one aspect of a multifaceted program, and its specific contribution to the positive results has yet to be established. For example, the Achievement Place programs (e.g. Fixsen, Phillips & Wolf, 1973) rely heavily on individualized counselling, peer-group self-government, and social skills training.

Successful reductions in recidivism and general improvement in community adjustment have also been reported for many behavioral group-home programs which have included female clients, but none have employed an adequate evaluation methodology (e.g. Wagner & Breitmeyer, 1975). Positive results in terms of posttreatment adjustment have been found for the Achievement Place programs which have provided methodologically sound studies and replications (Phillips, Phillips, Fixsen & Wolf, 1973). However, it has not been determined whether these positive results apply to the specific case of the female client.

The value of mobilizing the peer group in community-based behavioral programs is as important as it is in institutional programs. For example, improvements in grades and "drastic" reductions in tardiness and truancy have been reported for adolescent girls in a community-based residential program which provided rewards to each girl contingent on the school marks of the whole group. The success of the Achievement Place programs may be attributable in part to the system of self-government by the residents. Peer group input is a critical determinant of program outcome not only in behavioral programs but also in other treatment endeavors. For example, Kasakowski's (1976) analysis of improvements found in a study of adolescent offenders in a psychotherapeutic group home was attributable not to the therapy but to the influence of the peer group.

Contingency management and behavioral contracting have been employed in a large number of community programs for female offenders which have been reported to be successful in reducing such behavioral problems as fighting, vandalism, stealing (Tharp & Wetzell, 1969), truancy and school misconduct (Jesness, Allison, McCormic, Wedge & Young, 1975), and in improving academic achievement (McCombs, Filipczack, Friedman & Wodarski, 1978). Unfortunately, the methodology of all of these programs was not adequate to yield confidence in their posttreatment effects on antisocial behavior.

Contingency management has also been an integral component of several multifaceted programs which have been found to be highly successful in reducing recidivism. Thus, in the Buddy System, nonprofessional individuals are trained in applying contingency management skills to modify the problem behavior of delinquent youth. They are encouraged to form warm relationships with the youths assigned to them and to dispense social approval and material rewards contingent on their improved behavior. This approach was found, in a well-controlled study, to be highly effective in reducing school truancy and other assorted problem behaviors

(Fo & O'Donnell, 1974). Outcome results have also been positive. A group of 265 delinquent youths (boys and girls, ages ten to seventeen) were compared with 178 controls. Youths who had committed a major offense in the year prior to the project committed significantly fewer major offenses during the project year. Outcome appeared better for females, but a separate analysis by sex was precluded by the small number of female subjects (O'Donnell, Lydgate & Fo, 1980).

In another methodologically sound study, Walter & Mills (1980) substantially reduced arrests and institutionalization for a group of male (forty-four) and female (nine) delinquents through a sophisticated employment program which relied heavily on contingency contracting. Ninety percent of their subjects had no further arrests or institutionalization, whereas sixty-nine percent of controls had one or more arrests and fifty-two percent were institutionalized.

Contingency contracting was also used in the highly successful Complex Offender Project (Kloss, 1978; Kloss, 1980) in which intensive and individually programmed services were provided to high-risk offenders—those with psychological problems as well as criminal histories. The clients were probationers (aged eighteen to thirty) who had at least one previous juvenile or adult conviction, had previously received some form of psychiatric help or referral, and had a sporadic or poor employment record. Fifteen percent were female. During a sixteen-month follow-up, treated subjects had less involvement over time, whereas untreated control subjects gradually increased in the number of arrests, convictions and incarcerations. Treated clients had fewer charges after discharge from probation and also showed benefits compared with controls in enrollment and completion of educational programs, and in employment.

The O'Donnell et al. (1980), Kloss (1980), and Walter & Mills (1980) studies are model programs whose results merit replication with separate analyses with larger groups of female clients.

Behavioral contracting, then, appears to have considerable promise in community settings. However, a number of factors should be considered in establishing such programs. Contracts should be formal written agreements between the client and the agency which specify not only the personal, vocational, educational, or behavioral objectives which the client must achieve in specified periods of time, but also the rewards which will be forthcoming from the agency if the contract is fulfilled. The establishment of a contract requires careful negotiation and the acceptance of responsibility and commitment by both parties. Mutual agreement programs in which institutional release dates are made contingent on the completion of a contract, or voucher programs in which women earn a specified amount of credit to "purchase" services, may also be effective approaches, provided the foregoing conditions are met. Too often the contingencies are much too vague. The establishment of a contingency will not suffice; its effectiveness will depend on the nature of the relationship between client and treatment agent (Jesness et al., 1975), and on the consistency with which sanctions are enacted when the client breaks the contract (e.g. Copeman & Shaw, 1976). Finally, we must note that effective behavioral programs have employed contingency contracting as only one aspect of a multi-faceted approach; contingency contracting *as a single method* should not be expected to yield dramatic results.

Family Therapy

A number of studies have demonstrated that family factors are strong determinants of juvenile delinquency (e.g. Bahr, 1979; McCord, 1979; Wadsworth, 1979; Wilson, 1980). Parental criminality, poor supervision, punitive, erratic, or indulgent discipline and marital discord have all been associated with delinquency, as have quarreling, discord, hostile and negative interchanges, lack of parental warmth, poor communication, inadequate techniques for managing family crises or problems, and lack of consistency in rule-setting or rule enforcement. Several of these factors have also been found to be associated with recidivism (Maskin & Brookins, 1974). It seems reasonable, then, to expect that intervention with the family of delinquents may have value in modifying their antisocial behavior. The validity of this assumption has recently received impressive empirical support (Alexander & Parsons, 1973; Alexander, Barton, Schiaro & Parsons, 1976; Maskin, 1976; Arnold, Levine & Patterson, 1975; Eyeberg & Johnson, 1974; Johnson, 1977; Kent & O'Leary, 1976; Wade, Morton, Lind & Ferris, 1977).

Intervention with the family may be particularly indicated in the case of female offenders because female recidivists more frequently come from personally and socially disorganized families than do male recidivists (Ganzer & Sarason, 1973; Lambert & Madden, 1975; Maskin & Brookins, 1974; Sarason, 1978; Warren, 1979).

Several family intervention studies have included female delinquent subjects. These include the exemplary family therapy program of Alexander et al. (1973), an intensive multimodal approach that includes careful and detailed analysis of family interaction, modification of family communication, modelling, and contingency contracting. In this program parents are trained in negotiation techniques and in various behavioral management strategies. In a six-to-eighteen month follow-up of a methodologically elegant experimental study with eighty-six families (including forty-eight thirteen-to-sixteen-year-old female delinquents), their family therapy program was compared to client-centered family therapy groups, a psychodynamic treatment group, no-treatment controls, and countywide recidivism rates. Recidivism rates for the Alexander & Parsons family therapy group ranged from twenty-one percent to forty-seven percent less than for the other groups.

Another multifaceted program which included contingency contracting, training parents in negotiating and problem-solving techniques, and fostering clarity of communication among family members has also yielded impressive results (Wade et al., 1977). Compared to a seventy percent recidivism rate before the program, only ten percent of the adolescent offenders (mostly female) recidivated during a one-year follow-up. Moreover, no siblings of treated offenders appeared in juvenile court!

However, not all family therapy "works." Thus, Weathers & Liberman (1975) failed to find significant effects of their program on the behavior of recidivistic delinquents. The results of this study raise doubts about the efficacy of family intervention with offenders who have long histories of illegal behavior or come from extremely disorganized families or one-parent households. Byles & Maurice (1979) have reported the failure of a family therapy program to reduce the recidivism rate of 154 delinquent children (thirteen female) under fourteen years of age compared with that of a control group of delinquents who were not involved in family therapy. However, like most of the other reports which claim success for "family counselling" in corrections, they fail to describe the specifics of the program, the quality and training of the therapists . . . or the details of the evaluation!

The evidence of the importance of family variables in female delinquency and the success of some studies suggests that emphasis should be placed on family intervention with adolescent female offenders, particularly in terms of programs which focus on training, various communication skills and interpersonal problem-solving skills.

Recreation

The value of recreation as a way of occupying time, releasing tension, and improving physical and emotional well-being has long been recognized. However, recreational facilities and programs, including sports, leisure activities, libraries, games, etc., in most prisons for women are much more limited than they are in men's prisons (American Bar Association, 1976). Too often, television, knitting, and sewing are the only recreation available (Glick & Neto, 1977).

Education

The importance of correctional educational programs is suggested by several studies which have found that the vast majority of institutionalized female offenders have low educational attainment. Reading levels below the fifth grade (functional illiteracy) have been found in approximately fifteen percent of this population (News Notes, 1975). Close to sixty percent of the inmates in some institutions are high school dropouts (Glick & Neto, 1977). However, the educational level of female offenders varies greatly. In Glick & Neto's (1977) survey of United States institutions, "fourteen percent had not gone beyond grade eight . . . forty percent had a high school education or better."

Although many institutions offer educational programs ranging from literacy training to postsecondary courses, only a small proportion of the inmates enroll in such programs. One survey of United States prisons found that eighty-three percent provided educational programs, but only about ten percent of the offenders were participating in them (News Notes, 1975). Surveys also indicate that, particularly at the postsecondary level, educational programs are, in general, less accessible to females than to males (Chapman, 1980; Roundtree & Faily, 1980).

There have been very few adequate evaluations of the effectiveness of educational programs for females. As Bell (1977) concluded on the basis of his review of correctional educational programs,

> . . . little, if any, attention has been given to the measurement . . . of post-program followup, post-release followup, or recidivism rates in the evaluations of correctional education programs . . . the quality, effectiveness, and purpose of the evaluations may be, at best, questionable and, at worst, meaningless.
>
> (Bell, 1977, p. 93-94)

Interestingly, one of the most frequently quoted studies indicated that recidivism was unrelated to education in a women's correctional center (Johnson, Shearon & Britton, 1974). However, neither this nor any of the other outcome "studies" employed a methodology which could enable any conclusions beyond conjecture.

Many shortcomings in educational programs and in their service delivery have been noted. The most common is that of low offender motivation and participation. However, there are others which have considerable significance and may well, in turn, influence offender motivation:

- compromising of program quality and availability to the demands of security;
- low budgets (Bell reported that in 1970 less than one percent of prison budgets were available for education);
- hostility of prison staff towards education for inmates;
- ad hoc program development – education was not integrated with other programs, and had no articulated philosophy or goal;
- poor quality and inadequate training of teachers;
- inadequate materials, resources and facilities; and
- limited incentives for participation.

In recent years a general trend in correctional education programs for females is a reduced emphasis on regular academic education and an increased focus on social education, including training in life skills or job-related skills such as basic applied mathematics, communication, health and nutrition, money management, interpersonal relations, parenting, and child management.

The available research on correctional education for women provides little direction for policy-makers. Priority needs to be placed on developing a rationale for policy decisions regarding correctional education, evaluating programs for quality and efficacy, and examining means of improving offender participation. It must be noted that a common characteristic of most effective correctional programs is an educational as opposed to a therapeutic approach to offender change and development (Ross, 1982). As will be discussed in a later section, programs which foster development of social-cognitive skills, particularly in social perspective-taking, interpersonal understanding, and problem-solving may be as essential to positive correctional outcome with female offenders as they have been with male offenders. Such skills can be taught directly through specific cognitive training (Ross & Fabiano, 1985), or they can be included as an integral part of various regular academic programs (Duguid, 1981; Thomas, 1981).

Vocational Training and Employment Services

> *Many people, including rehabilitation specialists, accept the assumption that a woman is usually supported by a man, is suited only for certain jobs, and if given a choice, would rather stay home with her children than work.*
>
> (American Bar Association, 1976, p. 1).

In contrast to the early literature, which attempted to explain crime by females in terms of anatomical, physiological, or psychopathological factors, recent reports have pointed to economic factors as the major determinant of their criminal activity (American Bar Association, 1975; Chapman, 1980; Milton et al., 1976; Spencer & Berecochea, 1972). Female offenders, at least incarcerated ones, tend to be poor, undereducated, and lacking vocational skills which might equip them to earn a salary that would allow self-sufficiency. However, most will have to be self-supporting (Haft, 1974; Skoler & McKeown, 1974; Velimesis, 1975).

Although many were employed before their offense, most were employed in unskilled domestic service jobs (Glick & Neto, 1977) and, without training, will likely continue to be limited to similar positions, which are unlikely to provide them with the economic means for independent living. This is particularly the case if they must support their children (Glick & Neto, 1977). Employment with adequate salary appears to be a critical determinant of successful rehabilitation (American Bar Association, 1975; Lambert & Madden, 1975).

Most recent reports on the female offender have called for expanded opportunities for vocational training (American Bar Association, 1975; Milton et al., 1976; 1977; Gibson, 1976; Haft, 1974; Potter, 1979; North, 1975; Velimesis, 1975). In most instances, the reports have demanded only equality of treatment with males. In general, institutions for male offenders have more and better vocational programs than do institutions housing women (e.g. American Bar Association, 1975, 1976; Haft, 1974; Potter, 1979). A survey of adult institutions in the U.S. found an average of ten vocational training programs per institution for incarcerated men compared to 2.7 programs for women (Arditi & Goldberg, 1973). A survey of juvenile institutions found that the average number of vocational training programs for boys was 5.5; for girls, 3.3 (Milton et al., 1977).

However, steady employment may be a critical factor in rehabilitation, as indicated by studies such as that of Lambert & Madden (1976), which found that in comparison with a forty-six percent recidivism rate for adult female offenders with a prior criminal history, those who maintained steady employment after release from institution had a recidivism rate of only fifteen percent.

• **Outcome research:** Evaluations of vocational training programs for male offenders have typically concluded that such programs have little effect on postprogram employment performance or criminal behavior (Cook, 1975). There have been very few evaluations of vocational programs for female offenders. The few research studies which have been conducted have not shown clear relationships between vocational program participation and subsequent employment or recidivism.

Spencer Berecochea (1972) evaluated the ceramics, cosmetology, power sewing, landscaping, vocational housekeeping and nurses-aid training at the California Institution for Women. It was found that fewer than one-third of the 225 women were employed in the trades for which they had been trained in prison. At a twelve-month follow-up, only forty-three percent of the original study group was available for employment; the remainder had been returned to prison, absconded from parole, or were unavailable. Recidivism rates for women who had received vocational training and a comparison group were not significantly different. Vocational training appeared to have no effect on parole outcome.

A vocational program failed to demonstrate program effectiveness with female jail inmates (Ketterling, 1970). Four-month courses in grooming, child care, remedial reading, business filing, and vocational/group counselling were provided. When recidivism rates, employment status, and reliance on public assistance of the

102 participants were compared with 108 women who did not participate, *no* statistically significant differences were found between the two groups.

Analysis of Failure

Rather than simply concluding that the negative results of two studies establish that vocational training "does not work," it may be helpful to examine some of the reasons for the possible failure of such programs.

• **Service or lip-service?** It has been noted that in many instances, the duration and quality of training is inadequate; often it is vocational training in name only.

In many institutions, there is a high correlation between the housekeeping needs of the institution (food services, laundry, cleaning, sewing) and the "vocational training" offered (Velimesis, 1975; Gibson, 1973; Potter, 1979; North, 1975). Many work assignments which are really designed to benefit the budget of the institution and provide for its maintenance are euphemized as vocational training. Thus scrubbing floors is called "vocational laundry"; kitchen duty is called "training in quantity cooking." Sewing American flags has been called "social education." Watching TV has even been called "training in leisure-time activity." Potter (1979) reports on an eight-week program in "cashier merchandising," a dressed-up version of grocery store checking. Commercial supermarkets train cashiers on the job for such work in two or three days!

• **Keeping house:** As well as serving institutional needs, vocational programs often emphasize a restrictive domestic role for women:

> Many women's institutions pride themselves in turning out good housekeepers; the emphasis is on behaving like a "lady" or looking attractive and keeping things clean and neat.
>
> (Haft, 1974, p. 4)

Skills developed in this way may be largely irrelevant to those required in the labor market and are unlikely to yield the discharged offender an adequate salary.

Programs which actually provide vocational training usually are limited to training for jobs traditionally held by women that are generally not well paid (Gibson, 1973; Velimesis, 1975). As Haft (1974) has noted:

> In those institutions where vocational training programs have been established for female offenders, they are almost always limited to training women as domestics or other "women's" occupations, such as hairdressing, typing and sewing ... men may receive training in such higher paying occupations as auto repair, electronics, radio and television repair, printing, baking and carpentry.

In institutions for female juveniles, the most frequently offered programs were: cosmetology (56.2 percent); clerical (56.2 percent); nurses' aide instruction (50 percent) and food services (37.5 percent). In comparison, facilities for boys offered programs like auto mechanics, small engine repair, and welding (Milton et al., 1977).

- **Irrelevant training:** The kind of training commonly available provides skills which are not in demand (Milton et al., 1976). Few jurisdictions appear to plan on the basis of job market demand. Moreover, the qualifications received through institutional training are often not acceptable to community employers. While there is an increasing use of accreditation of programs, this represents a fairly recent development.
- **Retraining:** Ironically, more than fifty percent of adult female offenders have had prior training in the same fields that are typically taught in correctional institutions—cosmetology, clerical, and nursing (Glick & Neto, 1977).
- **Insufficient training:** Many programs fail to raise the vocational level of trainees from unskilled to skilled or semiskilled status (Spencer & Berecochea, 1971).
- **Someday he'll come along ...":** The primary goals of programs for female prisoners is often teaching "femininity"—"how to walk, talk and carry themselves" (Potter, 1978). In part, the emphasis on "femininity" is related to the view that the criminal behavior of female offenders indicates that they have failed to conform to their role as females and, therefore, must be trained for that role. More often, it reflects the view that the only hope for female offenders is marriage.

> By and by, three or four years from now, some nice fellow will come along, and you will love him, and he will love you, and you will get married, and live right. That ought to be the aim of a girl like you, to look forward to the time you have a good home and a good man.
>
> (A judge, quoted in Schlossman & Wallach, 1978, p.74.)

The goal of many correctional programs is marriage. This goal is shared by many of the women themselves; Gibson (1976) noted that "Instead of seeking the independence of a job skill, they seek 'someone' they can depend on."

For most adult female offenders, this fantasy is in stark contrast to reality. They will most likely be cast in the role of breadwinner, for themselves and also for their children (Velimesis, 1975).

> These...programs completely fail to recognize that on release the women will have to be the sole support of themselves, and in all probability an average of two children, and that certification as a clerk-typist does not provide sufficient income to meet these responsibilities.
> (Miller, 1977, p. 149)

The juvenile offender often has a similar dream for her future: a future of homemaking and child-rearing while supported by a husband. In view of current statistics and the likelihood of becoming a single parent, this dream is unrealistic (Milton, et al., 1977). This vision of the female role and way of life is becoming less and less tenable, for women in general as well as for the offender. Even in a two-parent family, the working mother is rapidly becoming the norm (Uzoka, 1979).

• **Discriminatory employment:** The female offender attempts to enter the labor market with at least two handicaps: her sex and her record.

> Because she is *female* she suffers from a number of well-documented discriminatory practices which affect all women who want to work—less pay for equal work; less opportunity to enter the better paying blue-collar job market; more credit problems...and fewer support services such as child care to allow her job flexibility. Because she is an *offender* she suffers from the prejudice of prospective employers; she is blocked from obtaining a license for many occupations; she is considered *unqualified* in the language of much civil service legislation for state and city employment; and she has problems in all jobs which require bonding.
> (Milton, et al., 1976, p. 35)

• **Motivation:** It has also been noted that the training options provided within the institution may not meet the vocational needs or interests of the participants. Few of the women enrolled in courses intend to pursue these occupations as a career, but seldom are they asked what they would like to work at before the courses are established for them.

• **Salaries:** Finally, the jobs for which women have been trained, if they can find employment, do not often pay well enough to meet basic financial obligations. Prostitution or property crime may be more lucrative alternatives (Haft, 1974).

Nontraditional Occupations

To remedy the apparent failure of conventional approaches and to provide female offenders with marketable skills that yield a good rate of pay, some jurisdictions have instituted training in occupations which have not been traditionally entered by women. In many settings, programs initially developed for men have been made available to female offenders as well – for example, carpentry, welding, and heavy equipment operation (Potter, 1979). In a few prisons for women, and in community-based facilities, programs have been developed specifically for women in a variety of nontraditional jobs, e.g. automechanics, electrical maintenance, plumbing, welding, and steam-fitting.

The benefits of such training may be substantial. For example, Hargrove & Faucett (1978) reported that women trained in nontraditional work (e.g. electronic technology, meat cutting, custodial work, printing, appliance repair) showed an increase from the average entry income of $3,924 per year to an average at follow-up of $10,547. The top earner was receiving $16,636 while the majority (seventy-five percent) were earning between $7,740 and $11,589. In terms of program completion and job maintenance, forty-one percent of the total group were successful in maintaining a placement for three months after a year in the program. Data on an additional nineteen percent were incomplete, but were considered likely to meet the criteria for the "successful" group. Twenty-three percent of the participants were excused before placement for such reasons as pregnancy, medical problems, drug or alcohol addiction, child-related difficulties, or mental retardation. Within this group, thirteen were assessed as being insufficiently mentally healthy to be trained for placement in demanding jobs. The clearly unsuccessful participants were terminated, for the most part, at the pretraining stage (eighteen percent). Only four women were fired by employers for poor job performance. Although follow-up data were not entirely complete, only four women were reported as recidivists.

Regrettably, there are no data comparing recidivism and employment outcomes for women trained and employed in nontraditional jobs to those trained and employed in more conventional "female" occupations. Certain kinds of women may be better risks for nontraditional job training and placement. While data are incomplete, it appears that women who have worked in any capacity previously, who are somewhat older than the average offender, and whose children are at least of school age may be "good risks." Personal qualities like emotional stability, independence, and persistence may also be important.

The proportion of female offenders involved in nontraditional programs has been small, but it may be at least as great as that found in the general population. Interestingly, a national study of United States correctional institutions found that only three percent of women offenders aspire to nontraditional jobs (Glick & Neto, 1977). This is an important caution for those who promote nontraditional training so enthusiastically; their enthusiasm may not be shared by the offenders.

Questions have been raised about the advisability of training female offenders to adopt nontraditional occupational and social roles since, it has been argued (Adler, 1975; cf Baunach & Murton, 1973; cf. Scutt, 1978), recent increases in crime rates for females are partly attributable to the "liberation" of females and their changed social roles. However, the relationship between women's liberation and crime has by no means been established (Adler & Simon, 1979; Weis, 1976) and as Velimesis (1975) suggests, "the jail and prison populations are psychologically about as far removed from the predominantly middle-class 'women's movement' as one could imagine."

Comprehensive Vocational Employment Programs

Neither vocational training nor job placement *alone* is likely to be an adequate rehabilitative service. An adequate program may require a combination of the following:

1. good-quality training of sufficient duration to ensure that the offender actually progresses from unskilled to skilled status;
2. training in skills for traditional or nontraditional vocations which are
    a) of interest to the offender,
    b) appropriate to her ability,
    c) in demand on the job market, and
    d) financially rewarding;
3. training not only in job-seeking but in *job-maintaining* skills (e.g. punctuality, relations with employers and employees);

4. job placement;
5. employer preparation; and
6. follow-up counselling.

The Hargrove & Faucett (1978) and the Walter & Mills (1980) projects provide models for such comprehensive programs.

Life Skills Training

Equipping female offenders with vocational skills may be a valuable, even an essential aspect of their rehabilitation, but there are other skills which are also required. Even if they were able to secure gainful employment, many offenders would be unable to maintain themselves adequately because they lack the basic life skills required to meet the demands of everyday living. Many need training in such essential skills as budgeting, banking, obtaining and discharging credit, purchasing, obtaining housing, household management, and the use of community resources. Many need to learn about medical and dental health, nutrition, birth control, child care and welfare. They need an understanding of legal rights and procedures, including marital rights, divorce, separation, child custody, and dealing with child abuse.

Reports by Chapman (1980), Glick & Neto (1977), Milton et al., (1976), Thomas (1981), provide descriptions of specific skills programs. None has been adequately evaluated.

Social Skills Training

Many female offenders also lack adequate interpersonal or social skills which would enable them to cope effectively in relating to employers, coworkers, social agency officials, or spouses. They may be excessively timid or aggressive in their social encounters, or they may evidence other inappropriate behaviors in their attempts to obtain what they need in interpersonal situations. Rather than viewing such characteristics as symptomatic of some underlying psychopathological condition requiring some form of "therapy," the recent literature tends to adopt a social learning viewpoint that views these problems as representing deficiencies in social skills which can be modified by training.

A number of reports have been presented of social skills training programs in which psychoeducational techniques (e.g. role-playing, modelling, direct classroom teaching) have been used to teach female offenders new social skills and how to use them to deal with interpersonal situations. The programs aim to develop skills which can serve as socially appropriate alternatives to antisocial behavior (e.g. Lowe & Stewart, 1983; Meler, Crotty & Dougherty, 1979). Unfortunately, we must report that no adequate evaluation of these programs has been provided.

Training in one social skill, assertiveness, has enjoyed considerable popularity with women in noncorrectional settings, but has seldom been evaluated with female offenders. Any enthusiasm one might have for assertiveness training should be somewhat tempered by the results of a recent study of this technique with institutionalized female delinquents (Knox, 1976). Thirty-six fourteen-to-sixteen-year-old girls were randomly assigned to one of three groups: an assertiveness training group, an attention control group which received a lecture on assertiveness, or a no-treatment control group. Although the assertiveness training group did become significantly more assertive than the other groups, this occurred only in the research setting—it did *not* generalize beyond the "laboratory." No significant differences were found in their behavior in the institution, nor did they become more likely to believe that they themselves, rather than others, determined their destiny.

Social skills training has been very popular in programs for delinquent boys (Goldstein, Sherman, Gershaw, Sprafkin & Gluck, 1978) but there is, as yet, no convincing evidence of its efficacy in reducing recidivism. Research on social skills training with offender populations indicates that whereas such programs may be successful in teaching skills in the training situation, their generalization to other situations often does not occur (Spence & Shepherd, 1983). Practitioners considering the use of social skills training with female offenders should consider Goldstein's "Structured Learning Therapy" program, which incorporates specified techniques for enhancing generalization (Goldstein, et al., 1978).

Cognitive Training

Many program managers have recognized the necessity of training female offenders in social skills and in life skills. However, there has been little recognition of the necessity of teaching another essential life skill: thinking.

A growing body of empirical research suggests that criminal behavior may be associated with developmental delays in the acquisition of a number of cognitive skills essential to social adaptation (Ross & Fabiano, 1983, I & II; 1985). Research has demonstrated that many offenders have inadequacies in a variety of cognitive functions. For example, they tend to be action-oriented, nonreflective, and impulsive. When faced with a problem or a temptation they immediately respond without stopping to think. They are less likely to *think* about problem situations than to *react* to them. They often "act out" without adequately analyzing the situation, or calculating the consequences of their action. Advice, warnings, or punishment often seem to have little impact on them because they fail to reflect on their past behavior and its effects.

Many offenders have never acquired critical reasoning skills, and they evidence a host of thinking errors. The most common of these is externalizing the blame for their actions onto other people or to circumstances "beyond their control." Many fail to consider or appreciate how their behavior and attitudes contribute to the problems they experience.

A number of studies have also demonstrated that many offenders are lacking in interpersonal problem-solving skills. They may evidence shortcomings in any or all of the following cognitive functions:

- the ability to recognize the potential for problems when people interact;
- the ability to generate alternative solutions;
- the ability to conceptualize the step-by-step means needed to reach their goals; and
- the ability to see the cause-and-effect relationship between their actions and other people's behavior.

Many have not progressed beyond an egocentric stage of cognitive development. They have not learned to distinguish between their own emotional states, thoughts, and views and those of other people. Lacking the ability to take the perspective of other people, they misread social expectations and misinterpret the actions and intentions of others. Their lack of awareness of or sensitivity to other people's thoughts or feelings severely impairs their ability to form acceptable relationships with people (including employers and spouses) and prevents them from developing appropriate means of dealing with interpersonal problems.

A United States task force survey (Glick & Neto, 1977) reported that inadequacies in cognitive functions represent an important aspect of the female offender profile: she has a perception that she has no control over what happens to her and thinks that she *must* depend on drugs, men, or social agencies (this may be a self-fulfilling prophecy). Many hold others responsible for their problems. Many lack an ability to think of options or alternatives and persist in self-defeating behaviors. Many have difficulty in planning and in decision-making and tend to act impulsively without adequate consideration of the consequences.

Such inadequacies in social reasoning do not necessarily reflect a lack in general intelligence. They may or may not be a consequence of neurological problems or learning disabilities. They may indicate only a lack of training. Such problems may be a result of a wide variety of environmental, familial, or cultural factors including abusive, overcontrolling, or undercontrolling parents, or a lack of exposure to individuals who model problem-solving skills or social perspective-taking. They may reflect inadequate training in communication or empathetic skills or a lack of reinforcement for problem-solving efforts at home or in school.

Research has demonstrated that a lack of such cognitive skills impairs the individual's capacity for effective social adjustment and places her at risk for a criminal adjustment. Research has also shown that remediation of the inadequacies is a *critical* factor in the rehabilitation of juvenile and adult offenders (Ross & Fabiano, 1982).

Correctional intervention programs which have included cognitive training techniques have been found, in methodologically impressive studies, to substantially reduce recidivism in both community and institutional settings (Ross & Fabiano, 1982; 1985). Several of these programs have included both male and female offenders (e.g. Fo & O'Donnell, 1975; Kloss, 1980; Phillips et al., 1973; Wade et al., 1977; Walter & Mills, 1980). In the following sections we describe some cognitive programs which have had particular success with female offenders; other cognitive programs which we recommend are described in Ross & Fabiano (1985).

• **Interpersonal cognitive problem-solving:** Many offenders may persist in maladaptive behaviors, not because of psychopathology, but because they simply have not acquired an adequate repertoire of reasoning or problem-solving skills which would enable them to respond in alternative ways to interpersonal and economic stress.

A number of programs have significantly reduced the recidivism of adolescent male and female offenders by utilizing programs specifically designed to teach them interpersonal cognitive problem-solving skills. For example, impressive reductions in illegal behavior were obtained for ten- to sixteen-year-old felons and misdemeanants who were trained in interpersonal and problem-solving skills in either a classroom/lecture format or a counselling arrangement (Collingwood, Douds & Williams, 1976). More than 1,200 male and female delinquents participated in this program. Significantly lower rearrest rates were found for treated delinquents when compared with groups who were referred to the program but did not receive training—a twenty-four percent rearrest/reconviction rate for the trained subjects compared to a fifty percent rate for the control group. The counsellors were mostly police officers who had been trained in Carkhuff's Human Resource Development Skills training model, a human relations training procedure that focuses on interpersonal problem-solving skills (Carkhuff, 1971).

• **Negotiation skills training:** A major facet of interpersonal problem-solving skills training is negotiation skills—learning how to analyze and deal effectively with interpersonal conflicts. The importance of such training has been viewed as essential to the success of a number of contingency contracting programs which have been found to be effective with delinquents (e.g. Jesness et al., 1975).

Training in negotiation skills and interpersonal problem-solving has also been employed in a number of effective programs which have involved training the offender's family. For example, Wade, et al., (1977) have demonstrated how male and female adolescents can be successfully diverted from further involvement in the juvenile justice system by involving their family in a short-term treatment program which teaches the family members how to negotiate with each other. Compared to a recidivism rate of approximately seventy percent for first-offender adolescents before the program, during the first year of the program, seventy-six percent did *not* recidivate. During the second year, eighty-three percent of adolescents did not recidivate. At a one-year follow-up only ten percent recidivated. Moreover, no siblings of the treated offenders appeared in juvenile court!

• **Role-playing and modelling:** Many offenders are deficient in role-taking skills. Their behavior problems may be a consequence of the fact that they have not developed cognitively beyond an egocentric view of the world; they have not learned to understand that others may have differing views from their own. Consequently, they tend to misinterpret the behavior of others. They may be unable to accurately assess other people's needs and feelings, or to predict how they will respond to them. They may also exercise poor social judgement.

A number of studies have successfully reduced the criminal activity of offenders by providing them with models who demonstrate prosocial means of solving interpersonal problems, or by providing them with role-playing opportunities (e.g. Chandler, 1980; Ollendick & Hersen, 1979; Ostrom, Steele, Rosenblood & Mirels, 1971; Sarason, 1978 [A]). Such training with female offenders may help them acquire new sets of self-instructions, teach them the benefits of cognitive rehearsal, enable them to recognize that there are alternative ways of dealing with problems, and help them to realize that other people's views and feelings may be different from their own.

• **CREST:** Role-playing is also used in the CREST project in combination with Rational Emotive Therapy and other cognitive techniques to focus on the thought processes and perceptions of male and female probationers and to modify their thinking errors and irrational associations. Several evaluations of this program have demonstrated that CREST graduates commit at least fifty percent fewer criminal acts than a variety of matched comparison groups and randomly assigned nontrained controls (Lee & Haynes, 1980). For example, one study showed that the total acts of misconduct for the CREST group declined by seventy-nine percent compared with a four percent decline for regular probationers. Another study found that monthly rates of misconduct for thirty delinquents in the CREST group dropped eighty-two percent, while the monthly rate for thirty-four controls on regular probation *rose* twenty-nine percent!

• **Grandview:** In Grandview, a maximum security institution in Ontario, Canada, role-playing and interpersonal problem-solving training engendered marked improvements in hard-core adolescent female offenders with a history of chronic and serious behavior problems and delinquency (Ross & McKay, 1979).

Major institutional behavior problems (assault, vandalism, self-mutilation, suicide gestures, and abscondence), which had been common and persistent before the program, were virtually eliminated. The postinstitutional adjustment of the girls was exceptional. During a nine-month follow-up period, their recidivism rate was 6.6 percent. The recidivism rate for a matched comparison group which received standard institutional care was thirty-three percent. Recidivism rates for three other matched comparison groups which were involved in behavior modification programs ranged from fifty-three percent to sixty-six percent.

These results were supported by an independent measure of postinstitutional adjustment, which found that the incidence of antisocial behavior reported by after-care officers was reduced between forty percent and sixty-five percent in comparison with matched controls.

The girls were trained in social learning (reinforcement) techniques and, rather than being the clients of a behavior modification program, they were persuaded to be its therapists. The entire program involved the girls in playing the role of mature, responsible, prosocial, caring individuals who were interested in understanding the behavior and feelings of others. They also continually observed the two program directors, who acted as therapist-models, and, in turn, the girls acted as models for their "clients."

In addition to role-playing and modelling, the program included direct training for each girl in interpersonal cognitive problem-solving. The program directors met frequently with each girl in individual or group sessions to discuss the behavior of the peer "clients." The meetings focused on helping the girls to understand their peers' feelings and behavior and helping them to consider various alternative ways of responding to their problem behaviors. The training was designed to develop the girls' empathetic understanding and to broaden their appreciation of the views of other people. It also taught them to stop and think about the consequences of their behavior in relation to their "clients" and to conceptualize alternative ways of interacting with them, rather than simply reacting to their behavior in their formerly characteristic impulsive, emotional, aggressive, and rigid ways.

The remarkable success of the program is probably attributable to many factors, but the cognitive aspects of the program appear to be central. The girls evidenced a marked change in their perception of themselves. They came to view themselves not as aggressive, hostile, antisocial and rebellious adolescents or as emotionally disordered patients, but as prosocial, altruistic helpers and teachers. Their self-esteem was greatly enhanced through the program, which continually reinforced their developing view of themselves as competent and worthwhile individuals. The program succeeded in having them change their behavior such that it was in accord with their revised self-perception.

• **Reasoning & rehabilitation:** The success of cognitively based programs for the general offender population suggests that it may be valuable to assess the cognitive functioning of female offenders and to involve them in cognitive training. A wide variety of programs and techniques have been developed to assess and to teach cognitive skills (Ross & Fabiano, 1985). They include self-instructional training, interpersonal cognitive problem-solving, negotiation skills training, alternative thinking, social perspective-taking, and means-end reasoning, among others. These techniques can be taught in many different situations, including institutions, halfway houses, and probation.

Moral Development Training

One of the effects of cognitive training may be an enhancement of the offender's ability to reason about moral issues or values. However, there is very little evidence that programs which specifically focus on the offender's moral reasoning and attempt to improve it by specific training (e.g. discussions of moral dilemmas) have convincingly reduced their illegal behavior. Even the positive results reported for the program for women offenders at the Niantic State Farm for Women (Kohlberg, Scharf & Hickey, 1971; Scharf & Hickey, 1976) have been called into question by Feldman's (1979) reexamination of the data, which led him to conclude that the program did *not* improve the inmates moral reasoning and did *not* lower the recidivism rates.

Reservations must be expressed, not only about moral development training in reducing recidivism, but also about whether it improves either the participants' values or their behavior. The relationship between moral reasoning and moral *values* is by no means clear; nor is the relationship between moral reasoning and moral *behavior*.

On the other hand, whereas discussion of moral dilemmas may not change one's moral values, it may serve to sensitize offenders to other people's views—to increase their social perspective-taking. Accordingly, moral development training, or values education, may be a useful adjunct to cognitive programs. *By itself* it is unlikely to have much impact. This may be because one's values can readily be compromised by a reality in which values are a luxury that one cannot afford; female offenders who lack the life skills or vocational skills that might enable them to maintain an adequate independent living and are unable to cope with intolerable social, financial, and family situations may find little comfort in their ability to reason about moral issues (including their own circumstances). More benefit may be gained through teaching the offender essential vocational, financial, and interpersonal problem-solving and cognitive skills which can enable her to cope with such circumstances—or escape from them. An extensive discussion of the value of moral development training can be found in Ross & Fabiano (1985).

Alcohol/Drug Abuse Programs

Treatment of substance abuse is an essential component in any comprehensive treatment program for female offenders. Alcohol and drug offenses are among the most common committed by females (e.g., Adams, 1978; Simon, 1975), and the criminal activities of many female offenders (particularly shoplifting, prostitution, burglary, and forgery) often serve as a means of supporting their addiction (Inciardi & Chambers, 1972). The number of female offenders who have alcohol-related behavioral or social problems, or who are addicted to alcohol, is substantial (James, Gosho & Wohl, 1979). A large number have drinking problems which seriously interfere with their ability to function socially in a noncriminal manner. Substance abuse is also a high risk factor in recidivism (Lambert & Madden, 1975).

Our literature search revealed a dearth of adequate studies of the effectiveness of substance abuse programs for female offenders. There are many descriptive reports of programs, but none provides data on outcome obtained through reliable evaluation research.

Correctional managers seeking to implement an effective substance abuse program for female offenders will find little guidance in the correctional research literature. Nor will they find much direction in the research literature on substance abuse programs for the broader female population (e.g., Cuskey & Wathey, 1980). Such programs often include offenders, but they typically fail to differentiate outcome for offender and nonoffender groups. Even if they did, the poor quality of evaluation would prohibit firm conclusions.

Relying on the literature on programs for male substance abusers is equally hazardous in view of the growing evidence that the development of abuse in women is considerably different (more rapid and severe) than it is in men (e.g., Wallgren & Barry, 1970); that female alcoholics drink for different reasons than do men (Wilsnack, 1973a, 1973b, 1976); that the onset of problem drinking is more likely to be related to stress (Beckman, 1975; Schuckit & Morrissey, 1976); and that women are less likely than men to have antisocial problems *before* the development of alcoholism (Tamerin, Toler & Harrington, 1976; Curlee, 1967). There are also reports that female alcoholics have a higher degree of psychiatric dysfunction (particularly depression and suicide attempts) than males and that sex-related hormonal factors are significantly related to the drinking experience of female alcoholics (Podolsky, 1963; Belfer, Shader, Carroll & Harmantz, 1971).

Differences have also been found between male and female alcohol addicts on factors (including substance choice) which might markedly influence the efficacy of treatment efforts (Bowker, 1978; James & d'Orban, 1970; Wiepert, d'Orban & Bewley, 1979). Moreover, alcohol treatment results appear to depend on the sex of the clients (Christenson & Swanson, 1974; Voegtlin & Broz, 1949; Fox & Smith, 1959; Pemberton, 1967). There are also differences between the sexes in the factors which are related to program outcome. Davis (1966), for example, found that voluntary commitment, dependency, and marital difficulty were correlated with positive outcome with women but not with men. Similarly, Bateman & Peterson (1972) found several educational, social, intellectual, and vocational variables which were correlated with posttreatment abstinence in women but not in men.

The outcome of treatment for drug addiction may also depend on the sex of the client. However, the evidence is equivocal about which do better: men (Christenson & Swanson, 1974) or women (Rosenthal et al., 1979). A recent study of 13,268 clients discharged from drug treatment programs found that "women experience more social prejudices than their male counterparts, and encounter greater barriers in completing treatment" (Rosenthal, Savoy, Greene & Spillane, 1979, p. 45).

Finally, we should note that some research has shown that "in males a history of delinquency has no significant bearing on the outcome of drug dependence, whereas in females a history of delinquency carries adverse prognostic significance" (Wiepert et al., 1979, p. 21).

Although there is a paucity of research on the efficacy of treatment of female addicts in correctional settings, the research demonstrating differences between male and female addicts suggests that they should be treated differentially. This suggestion is supported by a growing literature on the treatment of female deviants which has argued that effective programs for female addicts must be based on an awareness of the negative impact of addiction on feminine roles and self-image (Bahna & Gordon, 1978; Kaubin, 1974; Christenson & Swanson, 1974; DeLeon & Jainchill, 1980; Miller, Sevsig, Stocker & Campbell, 1973). They must also be sensitive to the female addict's special needs and difficulties in rehabilitation (e.g., Schultz, 1974; Velimesis, 1975; Mandel, Schulman & Monteiro, 1979; Levy & Doyle, 1974). Female offenders who are also addicts may need special programs (Ketterling, 1970), and it is possible that recent demands for nonsexist programs for female addicts will stimulate the provision of specialized programs and research for female *offender* addicts.

A comprehensive review of correctional programs for alcohol-abusing offenders notes that prognosis depends very strongly on the individual's alcohol history and social history. Specific assessment/classification procedures and differential treatment programs are recommended for male offenders (Ross & Lightfoot, 1985). In view of the apparent differences between male and female substance abusers, we cannot confidently recommend these procedures and programs for female offenders until their value has been established in controlled studies.

We must note that many, perhaps most, of the female offenders who evidence alcohol, drug, or multiple substance abuse have a number of other cognitive/emotional/behavioral and environmental/social problems which may be a cause (or a consequence) of their abuse; "their criminal behavior is a good deal more complex than simply obtaining drugs or money for drugs" (Weitzel & Blount, 1982, p. 271). In many cases their antisocial behavior predated their substance abuse (Martin, Cloninger & Guze, 1982). It is unwise to attempt to limit the treatment of these individuals to their drinking behavior without dealing with their other problems. Treatment of the alcohol-abusing offender must be comprehensive; we simply cannot treat one aspect of the offender while ignoring the others. It remains to be seen whether behavior therapy, cognitive training, guided group interaction, role modelling, and problem-solving skills training, which have been shown to have potential with male addicts (Hunt & Azrin, 1976; Sobell & Sobell, 1976; Platt, Labate & Wicks, 1977), also have value for female offender addicts.

Other Programs

There are, of course, many reports on various other program modalities, including art therapy (Levy, 1978); achievement motivation training (Footes, 1974); transactional analysis (Glick & Neto, 1977); reality therapy (Glasser, 1965); and nutritional therapy (Von Hilsheimer, et al., 1977). However, none of these includes an adequate evaluation.

3. Correctional Services

In this section we present a review of a number of correctional services which have been provided for female offenders and have been discussed in the literature.

Probation

Researchers and writers on the female offender have been so concerned with the conditions and the services provided in institutions that the reader of the literature might be led to believe that female offenders are all in prisons.

Given the characteristics of many of these institutions, the concern is appropriate. However, it has decreased interest in correctional services (or their absence) for the vast majority of female offenders who are not in prisons but in the community. This systematic disregard is particularly noticeable in Canada, where the interminable debate on the Kingston Prison for Women has drawn attention, interest, and possibly initiatives and funds from the much larger population of female offenders who are housed in provincial institutions, local jails, and community programs.

The oversight is well exemplified by the lack of research on the service which is most frequently provided for female offenders: probation. The popularity of probation as a disposition for female offenders certainly cannot be justified on empirical grounds; our search found few studies which provided any empirical data on the efficacy of probation. Although both effective and ineffective programs have been conducted with female subjects on probation, in no instance has the outcome of a program appeared to depend on the fact that the subjects were on probation.

Regular probation has seldom been the independent variable

in correctional research with female offenders. Usually regular probation is the control condition against which probation with some additional service is compared. Such studies enable us to determine only how regular probation fares against some specialized service. They do not provide needed information on how poorly or how well offenders who are placed on probation do as compared to offenders who receive additional services or do not receive probation.

One study which did compare probation with no probation was conducted with male and female adolescent first offenders who were referred to a probation department and assigned either to a group which was placed on "unofficial" probation (i.e., without formal adjudication) or to a control group which received no service (Venezia, 1972). A six-month follow-up revealed no significant differences in recidivism. The comparability of "unofficial" probation and regular probation is questionable, but this study suggests that the formal aspects of a probation disposition may be crucial. Another study failed to find significant advantage for probation in terms of recidivism when groups of male and female juvenile drug offenders were either placed on probation or given no intervention (San Diego Probation Department, 1971).

In much of the research on programs for female offenders which use a "regular probation" control group, researchers typically fail to specify what regular probation consists of. Probation services often include a number of integral program components which, in themselves, represent special intervention. In such circumstances it may be expecting too much to hope that the particular treatment program under study will significantly improve on "regular probation." Regular probation is not likely to be an appropriate no-treatment control. This problem is common to most correctional treatment research. Most of the control groups against which treatment programs are compared are likely to have received a fair degree of treatment as part of standard correctional services.

Although researchers have become disenchanted with the notion that reduced caseloads significantly augment the rehabilitative potency of probation, one study by Adams (1966) raises the possibility that caseload size for female offenders may be more important than for male offenders. Sixty-two girls assigned to officers with caseloads of fifteen subjects each, were subsequently committed to institutions less frequently and for shorter periods than were those whose probation officers had large caseloads (up to fifty). However, it appears that increasing the frequency of client contacts through reduced caseloads does not always have major impact on probation effectiveness. It appears that it is not the frequency of contact, but the nature of that contact that is most important.

Studies of probation with male offenders have clearly demonstrated the value of matching client, change agent, and program (e.g., Andrews, 1980; Barkwell, 1980). An important area for future research is not only to identify the characteristics of high- and low-risk female probationers but to examine the interaction between these characteristics and type of officer, type of supervision, and type of program. Research in this area has either failed to differentiate female and male offenders or has included too few female subjects to yield adequate data (e.g., Irish, 1977; Renner, 1975; Davies & Goodman, 1972).

The available research does indicate that female probationers present very different problems of supervision from males. Cunningham (1963), in an early descriptive study, noted that these problems are often so different that some officers find it impossible to apply their usual methods and consequently supervise them in a "formal routine manner" or "refer cases to another agency." Cunningham suggests that female probationers have different employment, recreational, and housing problems and concerns and are more likely to have problems associated with loneliness, dependency, and guilt. She also suggests that they are more likely to require counselling on marital problems and child care. Moreover, females may be inclined to form a dependent relationship on probation officers, to require more of their time, and to use manipulative techniques.

Cunningham's evidence for her conclusion is essentially experiential, but a recent study has presented some empirical support for some of her conclusions. Norland & Mann (1984) found sex differences in the kinds of probation violations reported for male and female probationers. Females were much less likely to be charged than males, in part because of the officer's paternalism and in part because the officer did not wish to jeopardize family relations. Men, when charged, tend to be charged for new offenses; women, when charged, for technical violations. The researchers suggest that this may be because women are "more troublesome":

> [females] threaten the routine patterns of contact between agents and clients . . . take up too much time . . . with what appear to be minor problems. . . . They may tend to develop a dependency relationship

> with the agent, which, from the latter's perspective, is inconsistent with the desired form of "amiable, superficial and brief" contacts.
> (Norland & Mann, 1984).

They also "tend to be emotional" and their problems are different—they focus on family, children, and welfare.

A major reason for the above problems is that agencies

> are not geared for working with women. There are but few halfway houses or shelters throughout the country for women. In the absence of such resources it is a practical and time-consuming problem for the probation officer to work out a good plan, especially for the detached woman without any family resources.
> (Cunningham, 1963).

Community Residential Services

There is a vast literature on community residences for female offenders (e.g., Milton et al., 1976; Arter, 1977; Contact, 1978; Garrell-Michaud, 1978; Marino, 1976; Lerman, Lerman, Dickson & Lagay, 1974; Miller & Montilla, 1977; Sojourn, 1977; Turner, 1969). This literature provides a wealth of information on the politics and funding of such establishments, and extensive details on the variety of facilities, services, and programs which can be provided. The literature also provides persuasive arguments for their use as alternatives to institutions. It provides *no* convincing evidence of their success in reducing the recidivism of their clients. Many reports are available describing positive program outcomes, but the lack of control groups prevents acceptance of these results (e.g., Kasowski, 1976; Marholin et al., 1975; Taylor, Goldstein, Singer & Tsaltas, 1976; Wagner & Breitmeyer, 1975; Upshur, 1975).

There is also no adequate evidence that placement in a residence is better than any other kind of community placement in reducing the recidivism of female offenders. One study found no differences between thirty-one girls placed directly in the community and twenty-six girls placed in a group home which provided a variety of educational and counselling services and contingency contracting (Minnesota Governor's Commission, 1973). Another study failed to find differences on a large number of measures between delinquents placed in a children's center with a behavior modification program and controls who lived at home (Handler, 1975). It appears that the ability of group homes to ameliorate behavior problems depends on whether the clients are male or female. Some studies suggest that they do better with boys (Birkenmayer, Polonoski, Pirs & McLaren, 1975); others that they do better with girls (Palmer, 1972). Presumably, much depends on which girls, which boys, and which group homes are involved.

The evaluation of community residences for female offenders is also inadequate to the task of ascertaining what program or service components should be provided to maximize the probability that the residence will be an effective alternative to other correctional measures or to leaving the offender alone. In this regard, research on the Achievement Place group homes has indicated that a number of program elements should be incorporated into such settings for adolescents: interpersonal cognitive problem-solving skills training, community support, peer group control and, where possible, family involvement. The Achievement Place model has been adopted in a wide variety of locales throughout North America and includes coed homes and at least one home for girls. Unfortunately, a separate analysis of the effectiveness of the model has not been reported for female delinquents.

Evidence of the efficacy of community residential centers for female offenders is less than convincing. This does not mean that they are less preferable to institutional placements. It only means that there is a lack of adequate research on this question and that one cannot argue for or against community residential placement of female offenders on empirical grounds.

Although some community residential settings may provide humane and economical alternatives to inadequate or abusive family homes or institutions, there is nothing *inherent* in a community residence which will ensure its effectiveness in terms of reducing the antisocial behavior of its clients or of protecting them from the many problems associated with institutions for adolescent females such as self-mutilation, violence, vandalism, and suicide gestures. These and other behaviors are often encouraged by an antisocial group culture in the residence, which can be just as negative, powerful, and damaging as that found in institutional settings (Elder, 1972; Turner, 1969). Research is urgently required to ascertain the prevalence of such problems and to determine what client, staff, and program characteristics are likely to obviate them. The adequacy of any setting does not depend only on its geography.

In short, although there is an abundance of reports suggesting *why* community residential placements should be successful, there are none which show whether, indeed, they are. However, there is no doubt that in many jurisdictions many female offenders are held in detention, not because they are a danger, but because there is a lack of alternative services or facilities.

Classification

Classification of female offenders is an impressively understudied process. This is probably attributable to the fact, that, in most jurisdictions, only one institution is available for female offenders – a situation which precludes classification as it is provided for males. In most instances it means that female offenders, regardless of their security needs, will be housed in the maximum security setting required for the small number of the female incarcerates who are security risks. The usual justification is that there are just not enough female inmates to make it practical to provide different settings with different security features. Classification proceeds, or is prohibited, by a lowest common denominator system – i.e., females are classified, not according to individual or group characteristics, but according to the security needs of the worst member of the inmate population.

The classification of offenders according to their needs for employment, education, and training is typically restricted by the same factor which limits classification by security: the lack of available alternatives.

The fact that female offenders do differ from each other on their characteristics and on their needs for housing and programming has been documented by a number of investigators (e.g., Warren, 1979; Pierce, Asarnow & Ross, 1978; Widom, 1978). It has also been demonstrated that the effectiveness of any correctional program is likely to depend on the client characteristics and on the nature of the supervision provided (e.g., Andrews & Kiessling, 1980; Hankinson, 1979).

There is some evidence that the assessment process which would be required in a classification program can itself lead to a reduction in illegal behavior. Cox, Carmichael & Dightman (1977) found a reduction in institution committals and recidivism among female (and male) delinquents who were processed by a community-based diagnostic program. An assessment was made of the client's history, personal strengths, and weaknesses and her family and environmental resources, and a referral was then made based directly on this assessment. During a ten-month follow-up, these diagnosed clients committed fewer and less serious offenses than a comparison group which did not receive assessment services.

At present there are no adequately researched classification/ assessment devices for institutionalized female offenders. Even if there were, their use for differential correctional intervention would probably be only an academic exercise, given the lack of variety in facilities, programs, and services.

Health Care

The medical and dental care of many female offenders has been episodic at best. Many have sought medical attention only when their health problems have reached a crisis stage; until then their health has been neglected. Accordingly, it is not surprising that many incarcerated females, particularly adolescents, are found to have many health problems (e.g. Ris & Dodge, 1972, 1973). Their medical problems often reflect ignorance, neglect, self-abusive behavior (including substance abuse), inadequate parental supervision and training, poor nutrition, poor health habits, limited access to health professionals . . . or indifference.

A health problem can add significantly to the other problems evidenced by offenders, such as low self-esteem, lack of employment skills, and limited motivation. Unless alleviated, health problems may serve as barriers to rehabilitation. Moreover, the offender who has not dealt with her own health problems may pass these problems on to her children. If her problems are a result of her own neglect, her children are likely to be neglected as well.

The widespread view that female inmates require more health care than males because they more often somatize their complaints has received scant attention by researchers. However, Wheeler (1978) has pointed out that psychosomatic problems are also very common among male inmates:

> Men also overburden sick call, complain of bad nerves, change symptoms while walking down the hall from one medical person to another, bad-mouth staff, demand medicine they don't need and fail to take medicine they do need, conceal real illnesses and threaten to sue as much as women do.

The provision of an adequate health care program may be essential not only to the offender's welfare but to her rehabilitation. Such a program should provide both health care services for the offender and health *education* to prepare her to assume responsibility for her own and her children's health.

•Health care service: Although systematic research on the health of women prisoners is sparse, a number of studies of specific institutions by Litt & Cohen (1974), Resnick & Shaw (1980) and by Ris & Dodge (1972, 1973) have identified some of the particular problems which are likely to be found among female adolescent inmates. They suggest that in addition to standard medical examinations, particular concern needs to be given to detection and treatment of sexually transmitted infections; cancer examinations (breast and pelvic); general gynecological care; prenatal, childbirth and postpartum care; abortion; menstrual problems; and problems associated with poor nutrition and the abuse of drugs.

Surveys have suggested that, in general, health care for female inmates tends to be disorganized and crisis-oriented. They often have less access to medical staff who are, typically, part-time and provide primarily emergency service (Glick & Neto, 1977; Sobel, 1980; Williams, 1978). In one survey it was noted that male inmates could obtain access to a medical doctor on a daily basis, whereas women inmates had sick-call only one half-day per week.

Many reports have recommended that correctional institutions recognize the importance of health care for female inmates and provide adequate services and facilities both in the institution and through nearby medical centers. Investigators have also made a number of specific recommendations for improving the organization of medical services and for responding to specific problems (Glick & Neto, 1977; Ris, 1975; Velimesis, 1981). For example, they have stressed that prison doctors should be female and have special training in gynecology. They suggest that the proper practice of medicine not be compromised by custody-security considerations. They have strongly urged that medical staff should be particularly concerned about the perils of dispensing tranquilizers and psychotropic medications, particularly when this is done not for the patient's physical or psychological well-being but for the well-being of the institution. Moreover, they have been highly critical of those settings in which the dispensing of drugs is done by untrained staff operating without rigorous pharmacological control. They have also condemned the use of tranquilizers as a substitute for programs.

•Premenstrual syndrome: Without entering into the highly controversial debate about the oft-assumed relationship between premenstrual syndrome (PMS) and criminal behavior (Hopson & Rosenfeld, 1984) we must note that many female offenders may report premenstrual symptoms (both physical and psychological) which may influence their adjustment and which should be seriously considered and carefully examined by both medical and social service staff. Treatment may require individually tailored pharmaceutical intervention (with due recognition of both short- and long-term side effects) and diet and exercise modifications, but should also include counselling and training designed to teach stress-reducing techniques, including relaxation, coping skills, and problem-solving.

•Pregnancy and abortion: Provision must be made for pregnant inmates in terms of prenatal care, delivery, and postnatal care. Local policies must be determined and clearly articulated on such matters as whether, where, and under what circumstances and rules abortion will be possible or delivery will take place, and what arrangements will be made concerning care of the infant. For example, in some settings, rooming-in at the hospital is arranged as are postpartum furloughs and foster-home visits for the mother. Careful consideration needs to be given to such matters both in view of the needs of the child (e.g. bonding) and the needs of the offender. Counselling should be provided relative to child care and parental rights and obligations. A wide range of approaches have been taken by various correctional agencies, ranging from pressuring the inmate to give the child up for adoption, to providing special facilities for housing inmates before and after childbirth. We will discuss these more fully in the section on child care.

•Health education: Many female offenders are ignorant of the basic functioning of their bodies and of rudimentary health care matters. Their ignorance may present problems not only for them but for their children. Accordingly, investigators have recommended that a systematic health education program be provided which would include general health information and specific training on sex and reproduction, nutrition, infant care, effects of drugs and chemicals, contraception, first aid, and obtaining medical services.

Correctional Child Care

In response to a recognition that many female offenders are mothers and that the majority are of childbearing age, many correctional agencies have provided special facilities or programs designed to impove parenting skills or decrease the extra hardships for incarcerated mothers and children that may result from their separation.

•**Number of mothers and children:** Estimates vary widely, but approximately fifty to seventy percent of female offenders are mothers (Gibbs, 1971; McGowan & Blumenthal, 1976; Rogers & Carey, 1979; Velemesis, 1975). Approximately fifty percent of the children are of preschool age (less than six); more than two-thirds are under ten or eleven. Many offenders have two or three children. Although in many cases, children were not in the care of the mother before her arrest, most of the offenders expressed concern for their children.

Although many inmate mothers express an interest in taking care of their children after their release, many do not do so when given the opportunity. This does not necessarily reflect a lack of interest. It often is determined by the women's lack of appropriate housing, money, and support services or by her view that she cannot provide adequate care. Nonetheless, the parenting needs of female offenders and their reaction to separation from their children must be carefully considered in planning programs and services both in institutions and in the community. In such planning they must consider not only the needs of the mothers but also the needs and best interests of the children.

The adjustment of the female offender will depend to a large extent on the support services which are available to her and her children, and on the degree to which she is able to cope with separation from her children, or with the demands of child care. Accordingly, we wish to describe some of the services and programs which have been suggested to respond to the foregoing concerns. First, it may be helpful briefly to review the effects of incarceration on mothers, on their children, and on family relationships. An extensive examination of these matters can be found in Stanton (1980).

•**Impact on mothers:** Investigators have reported that many inmate mothers experience not only loneliness but a variety of other negative effects from separation from their children. Some experience lowered self-esteem and guilt (from the feeling that they are failing their children). Some experience fears that their children will be taken away from them permanently. Some fear that they will lose their children's affection since they might form bonds with substitute parents, or because time might fade their memory of their mother. Some fear that their separation will be viewed as rejection, or that substitute parents will turn their children against them or prevent their return to her after release. A major identity crisis may be engendered for those women whose identity was defined primarily in terms of their mothering role. The postinstitutional adaptation problems facing the released offender may be greatly magnified for the mother who must handle, not only her own problems, but also the problems of her children, which may have been magnified by their separation or by inadequate care received while the mother was imprisoned.

Some mothers may experience incarceration as an escape from the stresses they have experienced in child care. However, many subtle and not-so-subtle pressures are likely to be brought to bear on their parental responsibilities. Whether they do or do not experience debilitating anxiety over separation from their children, their concern may preoccupy them so much that they lack interest in other issues such as vocational preparation, and making realistic life plans (Buckles & Fazia, 1973).

It has been demonstrated that loss of an important relationship may have a significant effect on intra-institutional adjustment and on the eventual outcome for the female offender. Family ties are among the most important factors in successful rehabilitation (American Bar Association, 1975). There is a remarkably consistent positive relationship between the strength of family ties and success on parole or reduced recidivism (McGowan & Blumenthal, 1976; Lambert & Madden, 1975; Kirkstra, 1967).

•**Impact on the child:** There are many reports in the literature which suggest that children may be adversely affected by their mother's incarceration (possibly experiencing prolonged separation anxiety, loneliness, confusion, fear, and anger as well as social rejection by neighbors and peers) but there is very little empirical evidence of this possibility (Gibbs, 1971; Miller, 1974; Rogers & Carey, 1979). Although there is evidence of a relationship between delinquency and parental criminality, the specific criminogenic influence of parental incarceration is a possibility which has seldom been studied (Wayson, 1975). The possibility that in some instances the child may benefit by separation from a harmful relationship is seldom mentioned. The extent of possible harm or benefit to the child may be related to the child's age and personality, the nature of the mother/child relationship, the cause and duration of the separation, and the quality of substitute care provided. Ironically, the adequacy of the mothering provided by parent substitutes (foster parents, relatives, etc.) is seldom discussed.

It should also be noted that incarceration of the mother does not represent a unique situation in terms of mother-child separation. Research has found that about twenty-five percent of female offenders did not have their children living with them when arrested and that more than fifty percent of inmate mothers have previously left their children in the care of others for extended periods of time. Moreover, before their arrest, many inmate mothers had lost or given up custody of their children for various reasons, and many others had transferred responsibility for raising their children to their own mothers or relatives (Glick & Neto, 1977; McGowan & Blumenthal, 1978).

•**Impact on the family relationship:** The effect of the mother's involvement in the criminal justice system on the mother-child relationship is not clear. In part this is because little is known about the quality of the mother-child relationship before arrest. For many offenders and their children, family breakdown may have occurred long before the mother's arrest or incarceration. It has been suggested that family breakdown may be just one of a multitude of social adjustment problems (economic, emotional, marital) related to criminal behavior in women (Rogers & Carey, 1979; McGowan and Blumenthal, 1976; Gibbs, 1971). However, regardless of the cause or the timing of the family breakdown,

> . . . women prisoners and their children are families very much at risk; unless there is some positive intervention, the incarceration of a mother is likely to create not only temporary distress for the child, but also long-term strains on the mother-child relationship.
>
> (McGowan & Blumenthal, 1976, p. 127)

•**Policy implications:** Clearly, no firm generalizations should be made about the effects of incarceration on either the inmate mother, her children, or the quality of their relationship. However, the familial responsibilities of inmate mothers and the best interests of their children should be considered at each point in the criminal justice decision-making process. In most instances this will require individual assessment. Some offenders may, indeed, use "my children, my children" as a ruse for leniency from the parole board and other correctional authorities (Baunach, 1982), but many others experience sincere and grave concern for their children. Moreover, their adjustment (and their children's) may depend on the services and programs provided for them.

A focus for research efforts must be to determine the extent to which inmate mothers actually reunite with their children after release, how many do so successfully, and what factors determine successful reuniting.

•**Placement:** The most prevalent arrangement for children of incarcerated female offenders is placement with relatives (seldom with fathers). Foster care seems to be used for placement for ten to twelve percent of the children (Rogers & Carey, 1979; McGowan & Blumenthal, 1976; Skoler & McKeown, 1974). However, somewhat more than this proportion may have been removed from the mother's care *prior* to her arrest.

Although some studies indicate that incarceration of the mother usually does not result in a disruption in the physical environment for her children (McGowan & Blumenthal, 1976), others report that, although the majority of children previously living with their mothers are placed with relatives, this represents a change in physical environment for sixty percent of the children (Rogers & Carey, 1979).

•**Contact during incarceration:** The great majority of women (eighty percent) maintain some contact with their children while in prison (McGowan & Blumenthal, 1976). However, two-thirds of the incarcerated mothers do not actually see their children while imprisoned (Rogers & Carey, 1979).

Although institutional facilities and regulations vary, a number of common concerns about children's visits have been expressed. Particularly where institutions are distant from the offender's home community, transportation may present insurmountable difficulties in terms of cost and time. Substitute caretakers may feel that a visit to a prison is inappropriate for the child. Some may not allow visits because they have strong negative feelings about the child's mother.

The rules in some institutions severely limit the frequency of visting by children. Many prohibit physical contact. Inmates and children may find visiting through glass or screens or with telephones particularly stressful.

In recent years many correctional agencies have paid increasing attention to the needs of inmate mothers and their children. Many institutions have liberalized their visiting regulations, allowed more telephone calls between mother and child, provided better facilities for visits, and initiated a wide variety of services designed to foster greater frequency and improved quality of contact between mother and child. Some allow children to visit on weekends whenever they wish and to stay overnight in the inmate mother's room. Some allow children to stay with their mothers for several days at a time. In some instances mothers may keep their children (up to age four) in prison with them. A woman's prison in Germany ("Prisons for Moms and Kids") allows inmate mothers and children (under seven) to live together in prison in a special wing. The prison yard is now a playground. While the mother works, the children are cared for by nurses. The children eat with their mothers and share their "spacious cells."

The variety of arrangements is a reflection of the complex social and moral issues involved in the question of whether children should be separated from their mothers or exposed to prisons. Concern must be given to questions such as the effects of such visits on the mother and the child when the visit ends, the feelings of other inmate mothers who do not have contact with their children, the effects on the child of seeing the often frightening physical structure of prisons, and the possible long-term effects of the children's exposure to criminal models. There has been no adequate research on the effects on the children of living in a prison for short or long periods of time. Nor has there been research on separating children, particularly infants, from their mothers while they are in prison. A significant number of children have been separated from their mothers in their formative years, when an intimate relationship is essential to their development.

•**Community-based contact:** The literature indicates that the practice of allowing children to stay in prison has fallen into disfavor. Alternative arrangements include providing special facilities on institutional property where children can live in an apartment with their mothers on weekends without being incarcerated in the prison itself.

Community facilities and programs in which mothers and children live together under supervision have become more popular. Such programs are used in some instances as an alternative to prison for offender mothers, but more often they are provided as part of a furlough, home visit, or temporary release program. At least one institution has arranged a foster-home placement service in which children are placed in foster homes in close proximity to the prison, thereby enabling the inmate mother to maintain contact with her children and to be kept informed on their well-being.

In all of the foregoing programs it is possible, and advisable, that additional services be provided, such as supervision, counselling, consultation with child welfare workers or other support service agencies, and parent-teacher or parent-foster parent discussions. Such programs may have benefits for the child, who may feel that the mother and the social service agencies are working together (for once) for his/her benefit. The child obtains tangible proof that his/her mother cares, and they can maintain their relationship within the context of visits and activities that are integrated into daily living, rather than isolated events. For the mother, the programs may reduce anxiety; she knows who is caring for her child and how. Moreover, she is involved in decision-making about the welfare of her child and has increased opportunities to improve her child care skills in a way that is not detrimental to the child. She also has a "trial period" that brings to the forefront the realities of child-rearing. The agencies involved obtain an opportunity to observe the relationships and are less likely to get caught between foster parent and natural mothers.

Temporary release programs are perhaps the most common means of arranging contacts between the inmate mother and her children. Research indicates that they may not be the best. McCarthy's extensive study has indicated that inmate mothers tend to view temporary release only as "vacations from incarceration" (McCarthy, 1980; 1979). Many evidence no interest in assuming child care responsibilities during their release. Although the furloughs enable the mother to maintain contact with her children, many mothers view them only as opportunities for enjoyment, not as opportunities to engage in child care. McCarthy stresses the importance of the correctional agency ensuring that the mother realizes the visit is designed for her to assume parental responsibility, and preparing her for this through counselling and skills training.

•**Parenting skills training:** Training female offenders in parenting skills has become an integral component of many correctional services. Programs include training in nutrition, health care, child growth and development, and parent-child relations. They also include instruction on birth control, methods of discipline, welfare, budgeting, maternal rights, and the like.

Ideally, this training would be provided in a situation where the mother is with her own children in a community-based facility offering a supervised, structured-living arrangement with an explicit objective of improving the quality of family life. However, it is more likely to occur in a classroom situation. Some jurisdictions have provided nurseries and nursery schools on the institutional campus for children from the surrounding community and provide supervised training for offenders while they are serving as aids to the nursery school teachers.

Surprisingly, the literature contains little reference to programs wherein female inmates are engaged as volunteers for institutionalized children (e.g., the developmentally handicapped). The success of such programs with male offenders suggests that correctional managers might be well advised to examine their value for female inmates (Gendreau, Burke & Grant, 1980).

•**Support services:** Teaching parenting skills to offender mothers and arranging suitable contact between the mothers and their children may not be enough to ensure that their parenting responsibilities will be well met. Many need parenting skills to enable them to handle their responsibilities as mothers but, equally important, most will also need "survival skills" to enable them to function as the head of a household and as the principal or only wage earner.

Offender-mothers and their children are often "imprisoned in a morass of regulations, agencies, social services, and legal actions" (Chapman, 1980, p. 131). Most lack the knowledge and skills to deal with such matters and require information, support, advice, and advocacy. Most of all they need crisis intervention services and legal and financial aid. They need such counselling and support services, not only while incarcerated, but also when they are separated from their children at the time of arrest and when they return to their children after release.

They also need advice about what and how to tell their children about their separation:

> Many inmate mothers tell their young children that they are going to school or to work or to the hospital "for a while." If the children are too mature to accept these explanations without question or are likely to learn of their mother's true location and status from other sources, the mother must somehow convey to her children the meaning and significance of her confinement. This may be a difficult and delicate task, because it must be done without injuring the children's view of

their mother or generating fears that other loved ones similarly will be taken from them without warning.

(McCarthy, 1980)

•**Pregnant inmates:** All of the issues we have pointed out in the foregoing are magnified in the case of pregnant inmates who wish to keep their children. In addition to matters of health care, adoption and placement services, and counselling, correctional managers and child care agencies must address the issue of separating infants from their mothers in view of the importance of the early contact between mother and child and the long-term effects of a lack of "bonding" during their formative years.

•**Evaluation:** There is an almost total absence of evaluations of the effects of such child care programs or parenting skills training on either the offenders or the children. It is interesting to know that, for example, of the ninety-one mothers who went through the "Prison for Moms and Kids" in Germany (Greening, 1978), only one recidivated. However, information on recidivism of the mothers is of very limited value as a measure of the success of programs which have such far-reaching social and ethical ramifications for the correctional agency, for the mothers, and for the children.

•**Policy implications:** The primary recommendation we can make is that correctional agencies must carefully examine the financial, administrative, legal, political, ethical, and philosophical implications of their provision of (or failure to provide) child care and parenting services.

Obviously some basic research is required. It needs to be determined how many of the inmate mothers who plan to care for their children actually do so. The various programs and services need to be evaluated as to the degree to which they are beneficial to inmate mothers and whether they are beneficial to their children. Studies need to be conducted to determine whether and to what extent the various service options influence the mother-child relationship and whether they have an impact on recidivism.

The variability of data on such basic matters as the number of inmate mothers or the number and age of children necessitates local needs assessment. Also required is assessment of the offender's child care skills, the adequacy of alternative placements, and the reality of the individual's future plans.

There is no clear evidence that the female offender is by definition an inadequate mother or role model for her children. Some imprisoned for child abuse and/or neglect most probably are; others, whose children have been removed or placed in foster care prior to their incarceration, *may* also be. Incarceration per se does not prove that a parent is unfit. Some whose children are cared for primarily by relatives may have little genuine interest in taking on parental responsibilities. Still others may have the required nurturing ability and interest to acquire such skills. The prevalence of family breakdown, evidenced by the number of children not in their mothers' care prior to incarceration, might suggest that many are not "good risks."

Finally, we must ask whether the criminal justice system, rather than providing programs, services, and facilities such as nursery schools on institutional property, might be wiser in the first place to keep the female offenders in the community with appropriate supervision, care and training.

Special consideration needs to be given to programs for women who have evidenced child abuse. Even if these women are separated from their children by incarceration, there is little to prevent them from having children in the future.

The following, adapted from McGowan & Blumenthal (1976), summarizes the services and programs which correctional agencies may wish to consider.

- Counselling re: separation, child care laws and agencies, support services, foster care.
- Communication: providing information for mothers on the well-being of their children through contact with child care agencies.
- Liberalized visiting facilities and arrangements: more visits, telephone calls, and furloughs than currently allowed; longer visiting hours, telephone calls, and furloughs; "contact" visits; more appropriate setting for visits on prison grounds; fewer correctional staff present during visits; visiting days and times varied so that it is easier for caretakers to bring children; transportation directly supplied or caretakers reimbursed for the costs of transportation; systems whereby caretakers pool transportation for visits by children; caretakers and foster parents urged to bring children to visit; more planned activities for mothers and children during visits; picnics and other family get-togethers; group overnight outings for mothers and children; opportunity to take pictures of children when they visit; indoor playrooms and outdoor playgrounds for children during visits.
- Housing for children: nurseries on prison grounds; separate apartments on prison grounds for mothers and their children; cottages or apartments located near, but not on, prison grounds for women and/or their children.

•Substitute caretakers: information for mothers concerning foster homes; foster homes and group homes for children located close to prison; improved relationships between foster parents and inmate mothers accomplished by arranging for them to meet prior to the child's placement; encouraging regular visiting and organizing ongoing discussion between mother and caretaker; visits to mother by child's caseworker.

•Parent education: child development, family planning, nutrition, discipline, family relationships; provision of nursery school training.

•Postrelease services: counselling (to ease readjustment of parent and child); housing; work opportunities; financial support, babysitters; legal services and information regarding parental rights; legal representation in custody and divorce cases; medical services; information regarding public assistance.

•Services for children in the community: special educational programs; day-care services; preschool programs; liaison between school personnel and mothers.

Work/Training Release

Temporary release programs are being increasingly used for female offenders as a way for correctional agencies to increase the number and variety of educational or occupational training programs and to provide essential work experience. Rather than incurring the considerable costs for equipment and trainers that are required for training programs for a small number of inmates in an institution, arrangements are made with community schools, training centers, or industries to provide these services. A number of living/working arrangements can be provided, including institutional stay with day release, temporary release to community correctional centers, halfway houses, and prerelease work centers, and conditional release on parole to attend classes or employment.

There has been very little research on these programs. However, a number of surveys have indicated their growing popularity (Chapman, 1980; Neto, 1981). It has been noted that management's use of work release is often a rather haphazard process without a clearly defined set of goals and objectives and without defined criteria for inmate selection. In most instances it is done on an individual case basis without an established policy. Often it is little more than a means of reducing overcrowding.

A study by Fine (1978) found that a small sample of women parolees who had participated in a work/training release program had a low rate of return to prison, but the study's methodology was inadequate to determine whether their "success" was related to the program or their selection as participants. Less support for work release was found in a study which found that rule violations in the institution increased considerably more among women on work release that among any other group in the institution (Faily & Roundtree, 1979). Unfortunately, there are no other adequate studies, and the shortcomings of the previous two studies leave us with little empirical information on the effectiveness of work/training release.

Although its popularity is growing, work release is still much less a possibility for women than men. This, perhaps, reflects a misperception that women have less need to become self-supporting than men and the unsubstantiated view that women are less likely to respond to such rehabilitative employment programs (Chapman, 1980). Crites (1976) has noted that work release is "a prime example of a reform pioneered by women and now scarcely available to them."

•**Policy implications:** The cost effectiveness of work/training release programs needs to be assessed. Such programs need to be provided as part of an established policy for vocational and educational programming in which work release is an integral part of a comprehensive program including vocational assessment, screening and selection, orientation, goal setting, vocational counselling, job-readiness training, vocational training, job search, development and placement, and support and follow-up services.

Mutual Agreement Programs

An increasing number of mutual agreement programs (MAPs) are being used in a number of United States settings. A MAP is a negotiated plan for early release which represents a contractual arrangement between the offender, the prison staff, and the parole board that she will be released if she successfully completes (within a specified time period) some specific vocational or educational goals which meet her needs (as assessed early in her sentence by the inmate in consultation with a MAP counsellor).

MAPs have many advantages. They provide clear contingencies for the offender so that she feels some control over her destiny; they reduce uncertainty; they may increase motivation and effort;

they provide the offender with a clear articulation of the purpose and objectives of her incarceration and provide her with some goals. On the other hand, they may place too much emphasis on the acquisition of vocational skills and underemphasize the importance in rehabilitation of improvement in social skills, attitudes, and values. Moreover, they may substantially reduce the freedom of parole boards in making decisions to release or not release on the basis of other factors. Whether the advantages outweigh the disadvantages has not been determined by empirical studies.

Vouchers

Another method of contracting with female offenders for the provision of vocational or educational services is through vouchers which they are given (sometimes contingent on their behavior). The vouchers can be used to purchase specified amounts of training, education, or other rehabilitative services in the community. Such systems give the offender access to diverse services available in her particular community and provide her with an active role (and responsibility) in determining which services best meet her needs. Vouchers help to make the principles of an opportunities model into a concrete reality.

Co-corrections

Co-corrections—the integration of male and female offenders in a shared institution—has been advocated in a large number of reports on female offenders. The possible advantages of co-corrections for women have been well articulated, but there are many less-publicized disadvantages which policymakers must recognize.

•**Program opportunities:** Relative to the program availability in most small women's prisons, the co-correctional prison may provide far more program opportunities for females by allowing them access to the usually greater number of recreational, vocational and educational programs which are usually available to the larger number of male offenders. However, the small number of women inmates often results in their interests and needs being subordinated to those of the men. Typically, the male-oriented programs are modified to meet some of the needs of women, not the reverse. Several studies have shown that many women do not take advantage of the opportunities provided in co-correctional institutions. This is, in part, because the atmosphere is male-oriented and the women perceive themselves as appendages (Chapman, 1979; Schweber, 1979). It is essential that correctional management attempt to modify the institutional climate in a way which makes integration real.

•**Geography:** Because most jurisdictions have only one women's prison, geography often limits the women's contact with family members. However, being housed closer to home in an integrated prison often means that the women must accept the same visiting rules as men. This can mean reduced frequency of visits and less freedom during the visits (less contact and more restrictions on children visiting).

•**Inmate deportment:** Many comments (but little persuasive data) suggest that women have a humanizing or calming effect on the prison atmosphere—that they reduce violence among the men, and improve their appearance, language, and general deportment (Ruback, 1975; Nacci, 1978). In this regard, critics of co-corrections have lamented corrections using women as an institutional control technique.

•**Normalizing:** It has been suggested that co-corrections helps to normalize the institution by eliminating the "unnatural" desegregation of the sexes. However, the ratio of males to females in co-corrections is typically far from "normal." Moreover, with very rare exceptions (e.g. Anderson, 1981), co-correctional institutions enact very stringent regulations on the nature of the contact permitted between male and female inmates, which clearly contradicts the normalizing supposedly achieved by the resumption of heterosexual activities in co-correctional settings. There is little evidence that co-corrections decreases homosexual activities in either males or females. As Ross & Hefferman (1977) report:

> [the] return to "Street Behavior" Syndrome is widespread in coed institutions. A pattern of relating to the opposite sex by day and the same sex by night. . . . Women continue their homosexual relationships for support and engage in heterosexual relations for financial purposes.

Critics have noted that co-corrections "normalizes" in another way—it places women in a minority situation in which their needs are subordinated in a male-dominated environment. There is nothing about a co-correctional institution which prohibits management from deciding in allotting programs and services to focus on the needs of the majority—the men. Thus, "co-ed is not co-equal." (Smykla, 1979). Particularly in jails, fears of mixing men and women frequently mean that women will not be allowed access to recreational or other programs.

It has been argued that what female offenders need is a women-centered environment (Anderson, 1978; Arditi et al., 1973). Many would suggest that it may, in fact, be therapeutic for them to be away from men, particularly male offenders. Interestingly, co-corrections is seldom recommended in reports on male offenders.

•**Community access:** Sacks (1978) has argued that most women's prisons are distant from community resources and that by housing female offenders in male institutions they gain access to such resources. Unfortunately co-correctional housing does not always lead to this effect because the male institutions which are converted or built for co-corrections are often even more isolated geographically than the women's prison. The purpose of changing to co-corrections often is not to provide greater program access, but to make better use of available bedspace, which is usually greater in institutions located in rural settings (Ross & Hefferman, 1977).

There are other disadvantages for women in co-correctional settings. As Wheeler (1978) has noted, they lose whatever advantages there are in *some* small institutions, such as better staff/inmate ratios. Moreover, in a larger co-correctional setting they may have much less freedom because their activities are more restricted and more closely watched to protect them or to prevent violation of sexual fraternization rules. Despite such rules, pregnancy may occur. Suspicions and jealousies of the inmates' spouses or friends in the community can also create major difficulties.

Women are likely not to be housed with medium or maximum security inmates but, rather, with minimum security inmates. Women classified as maximum security may be denied integration even within the integrated institution. They may find themselves in a "prison within a prison" (Haft, 1974).

Co-corrections may also place considerable pressure on the male inmates, not only in terms of the contact prohibitions, but in terms of problems associated with large numbers of men competing for the attention of a small number of females. Major restrictions may also be placed on the freedom of the male offenders.

There are, as yet, no adequate studies of the differential outcome of single sex and co-correctional institutions.

•**Policy implications:** Correctional managers must carefully weigh the benefits and disadvantages of co-corrections. It is regrettable that in their considerations they will be little aided by empirical data—conclusions about the effects of introducing co-corrections have seldom been based on systematic study (Smykla, 1980).

An alternative approach which has many of the merits of co-corrections and fewer of the shortcomings we have mentioned above is the "coordinate model" (Schweber, 1984). In this model women are housed in separate institutions but have access to programs and services (recreation, education, medical, etc.) available in a nearby men's institution or institutions. This enables management of both institutions to maintain their autonomy in terms of institutional control practices. It also provides the potential for greater opportunities for female offenders without compromising other aspects of their care and without costly duplication of services.

Parole

Many of the problems in supervising female probationers which have been reported are also found in supervising female parolees (DeVault, 1965; Spencer & Berecochea, 1972). Parole and probation for females are similar in another respect: lack of research (Pauze, 1972).

There is some research on the relationship between the likelihood of granting parole and the characteristics of women offenders. Bedford (1974) found that the likelihood of parole was higher for married women and women with dependent children than for single women without children. Women who maintained or evidenced plans to maintain relationships with children or husbands were also less likely to experience parole revocation (DeVault, 1965). Moreover, as in the case of probation, women are less likely than men to be revoked for a new offense, but two to three times more likely than men to be revoked for a violation of parole rules (Spencer & Berecochea, 1972).

In the case of adolescents, the risk of recidivism is greater for younger girls who have a longer history of delinquency, had accomplices when committing their offenses (Molof, 1970), had a previous commitment to a training school or a mental hospital, previous probation, poor education, and young age at first conviction. In the case of adults, risk also varied as a function of the type of crime, with homicide and manslaughter representing the lowest risk, forgery and fraud the highest. A history of drug use markedly lowered parole success. Poor parole outcome is also associated with homosexuality, low education, longer commitments, and social isolation (Bowker, 1978).

The results of one well-designed study raise serious doubts about the value of one aspect of parole with adolescent offenders: supervision. Offenders randomly assigned after parole from institutions to either supervision or nonsupervision did not differ in personal or community adjustment (Hudson, 1976).

Another study found that among 287 women offenders considered for parole, "good risk" women who were not parolled were reconvicted at a higher rate than expected, and at a much higher rate than "good risks" who were granted parole. The researcher argues that this demonstrates that being turned down has more negative impact than parole has positive impact. However, there is not enough evidence to reject the possibility that the poor performance of "good risks" who were turned down simply indicates that the parole board chose wisely.

Interestingly, in accord with our conclusions about the importance of social competence, the best predictor of success on parole has been found to be interpersonal skill—the ability to relate to people (Robinson, 1971).

Correctional Staff

It is, or at least should be, considered axiomatic that the effectiveness of any correctional program is strongly influenced by the characteristics and the quality of its staff. Programs which are operated by poorly selected, trained, motivated, or supervised staff should not be expected to "work" (Gendreau & Ross, 1979).

Although there have been many suggestions that more female staff should be enlisted both for line positions and management positions in corrections, the literature is concerned only with increasing their number, not with improving their quality. We found very little research on the characteristics of effective staff in programs for female offenders. However, there are several reports of studies of the characteristics of volunteers.

•**Volunteers:** The involvement of unpaid volunteer workers in correctional services for female offenders is widespread. Volunteers most frequently relate to female offenders in terms of recreational/leisure time activities, but many programs use volunteers (both male and female) to provide other services based on a one-to-one relationship, e.g. supportive counselling and academic tutoring.

The Sisters United program provides a model for such programs (Sykes & Green, 1978). Trained volunteers are matched with delinquent girls and involve them in various activities (e.g. arts/crafts; tutoring; sports; cultural events) four afternoons per week for six to twelve months. A cost-benefit analysis of this program has shown a recidivism rate of less than two percent at an annual average savings of $3,188 per girl over girls in state-related, community-based programs. The adequacy of the research is open to question, but these results should stimulate more carefully designed cost-benefit studies of volunteer services for delinquent girls and for adult female offenders.

Whereas many of the volunteer programs for female offenders focus on somewhat traditional feminine activities (home decorating, beauty care, dressmaking, etc.), there are several innovative programs which are noteworthy. For example, volunteers have played an important role in a therapeutic camping program which has reported impressive results. The Girls' Adventure Trails in Texas is a short-term diversion program in which delinquent girls participate in a four-week wilderness trip (Hovatter, 1979). During the trip, "reality oriented group techniques" are used to teach problem-solving, group cooperation, and responsibility. Unlike other therapeutic camping programs, this program includes a component for parents. While the girls are camping, their parents are involved in counselling designed to teach parenting skills which can help maintain the girl's changed behavior after she returns from the trip. Six months of follow-up counselling by trained volunteers is provided for the girl and her parents. Follow-up contact and the results of a two-year preliminary study of over 750 girls who have participated in the program suggest that "about two-thirds of the girls made significant attitude and behavioral improvements and were able to reasonably maintain their gains during the follow-up period." More rigorous evaluation of this program is warranted.

In another study, a comparison of female juvenile offenders on regular probation supervision with those receiving counselling services by volunteers showed *no* overall difference in rearrest rates, although the girls in the counselling group evidenced less serious offenses (Ganter, 1976). However, as this study and other studies of volunteer programs in corrections make clear, evaluating programs on the basis of "overall" rearrest rates is overly simplistic. Volunteers differ markedly in their ability to effect change in offenders (Andrews & Kiessling, 1980). Volunteers whose clients had low recidivism held attitudes which emphasized acceptance of their client's basic needs, worth, personal liberty, responsibility, and willingness to change; they were sensitive to the problems of adolescence and were willing to give information on contraception. The clients of more conservative volunteers who held these attitudes less strongly had much higher recidivism rates. However, as Andrews & Kiessling (1980) have pointed out, empathy, trust, and unconditional positive regard will not suffice to engender change unless the volunteer staff member also consistently enforces rules and models prosocial behavior.

Many effective volunteers are university students who, if well selected and trained, can serve as excellent models for adolescent offenders, partly because they are close in age and interests to the offender and partly because they can teach, by their example, prosocial means of acquiring the rewards they seek.

•**Service delivery:** An excellent service delivery model which has been used in several highly effective programs using university student volunteers is the "triad" model. This model increases the availability of low-cost services by having such services delivered directly to the clients, not by professional staff, but by students who have been trained by professionals and are supervised by more senior experienced students, who have also been trained and are directed by the professional. Since the consultants have minimal contact with the clients, this organizational plan can have important cost savings, which can be accomplished without lowering the quality of service. For example, Wade et al. (1977), with a paid staff of only one full time co-ordinator/counsellor and one half-time secretary, provided family therapy services to 321 families (including 63.8 percent female delinquents) in a four-year period with a recidivism rate of 14.7 percent, compared to a seventy percent rate the previous year. The direct services were provided by trained graduate students, who earned practicum course credits. The therapists in Alexander & Parsons' (1973) successful family therapy programs were also graduate students whose participation earned them practicum credits. Recidivism rates for their delinquent clients (including forty-eight females) were almost half the rate of those for no treatment controls.

Similarly, in the CREST project, Lee & Haynes (1980) deployed a small number of graduate students, paid as teaching assistants, to supervise a large number of other unpaid student volunteers, who provided counselling services to male and female probationers. The project yielded persistent and impressive benefits. The total acts of misconduct for the CREST group declined by seventy-nine percent, compared with a four percent decline for regular probationers. The average monthly rates of misconduct for thirty delinquents in the CREST group dropped eighty-two percent, while the monthly rate for controls on regular probation *rose* twenty-nine percent. In a twenty-four-month follow-up, fifty-nine percent of the CREST group sustained an offense-free record for the final eighteen-month period (Piercy & Lee, 1976).

A similar model has been used in programs involving paid, part-time nonprofessional behavior change agents. For example, in the "buddy system," impressive results have been obtained with female offenders using "buddies" who were recruited from the local community and trained in contingency management techniques and in established relationships with delinquent youths. "Buddies" could earn up to $144 a month contingent on their performance. Their training and supervision were provided by graduate students, who earned internship credits for their participation. The students, in turn, were under the direction of professionals—university faculty (Fo & O'Donnell, 1974; O'Donnell, Lydgate & Fo, 1980).

Nonprofessional staff have also played an important role as foster parents for delinquent youth. The selection, training, supervision, and effectiveness of foster parents for female delinquents has seldom been studied. The availability of suitable foster parents is also a recurrent problem, particularly in the case of female delinquents (Milton et al., 1977).

One of the most promising programs which we found was the PROCTOR program, a home-based detention program in which single young women were selected and trained to provide daily care and supervision for delinquent girls, aged thirteen to seventeen, in the proctor's house or apartment (McManus, 1976). Proctors provided services of the kind usually provided by child care or social workers and functioned as independent, self-employed subcontractors serving not only as caretakers and counsellors but as models of positive and self-sufficient lifestyles for women. Both descriptive data and a three-year evaluation attest to the success of the program, concluding that it had considerable value as an alternative to institutionalization, particularly for females who require close individual attention but reject parental-style supervision (Pappenfort & Shireman, 1976). The possibility of combining the PROCTOR model with the triad model in collaboration with a university program in which senior university students trained and supervised by professionals would serve as proctors should be explored.

•**Nonsexist staff:** Critics of correctional services have long lamented the fact that programs for female offenders have typically derived from sexist explanations of female criminality. Most have been conceived and conducted by males who do not understand women's problems or the social/political/economic causes of their problems, and/or by females who have perpetuated sex-role stereotypes for women (Feinman, 1979). It is argued that staff (both male and female) are required who will follow a nonsexist approach. The nonsexist staff member is aware of his/her values, rejects prescribed sex-role behavior and marriage as *the* treatment goal, denies anatomical explanations of behavior, and promotes autonomy for his/her client.

•**Models:** Research on the characteristics of effective staff in correctional programs suggests that the criteria for selection should stress social competence and the ability to model prosocial interpersonal problem-solving skills (Andrews & Kiessling, 1980; Ross & Fabiano, 1985). It is important that they possess those skills which many offenders lack—interpersonal cognitive problem-solving: self-control, social perspective-taking, alternative thinking, and means-end reasoning. They must be able to apply rules consistently in dealing with problematic behaviors, but in so doing they must be able to consider the effect of their actions on others and to conceptualize alternative ways of responding to them.

4. Policy Implications and Program Recommendations

Before making recommendations for policy formation and program development, we wish to reiterate a number of general conclusions which appear warranted by our analysis of reports on correctional services for female offenders.

•**The forgotten offenders:** Until very recently, and with very rare exceptions in the development of criminal justice programs and services, female offenders have been neglected. Correctional services in both institutional and community settings have been designed by men for men, who comprise more than ninety percent of the correctional population. The development of services for women is usually an afterthought; programs which are available for them are often extensions or "hand-me-downs" of programs established for males. Correctional facilities are often mere appendages (either figuratively or literally) of facilities designed for males.

•**Footnotes in the criminological literature:** Until 1975, female offenders were also largely ignored in the criminological literature. Most books on criminal justice devote less than a few paragraphs to female offenders. In many instances they are mentioned only in footnotes.

•**Program availability:** The available literature makes it clear that because of many political, economic, and ideological factors, correctional services and programs available for women are fewer, less varied, and of poorer quality than they are for men.

•Equal is not necessarily better: In recent years there has been an increasing pressure on correctional managers to provide more services for female offenders. Typically, the demand has been for equality with men in terms of program availability. The demand for equality may be warranted, but its achievement may serve to limit female offenders to the quantity, quality, and variety of services which are available to men – services which may not meet the needs of either group. Moreover, by focusing management's attention only on providing women with the same services as men, we may inadvertently succeed in marginalizing female offenders by increasing the likelihood that services for them will be mere extensions of services designed for men.

The demands for change are based on human rights and equal rights considerations, on sentiment and good intention; seldom are they based on an adequate appraisal of the characteristics of female offenders and their circumstances. Rarely has there been an objective appraisal of the value of the programs and services which are recommended.

•Program efficacy: The evaluation of programs for female offenders has also been largely ignored by researchers. Although there are innumerable reports of popular and, sometimes, innovative programs, the typical program description is a descriptive narrative about a program venture whose evaluation is impressionistic and based only on personal testimony and anecdote. There are very few carefully designed studies which could provide useful objective data for policy planning.

Most research on the treatment of offenders does not include female subjects. Projects which do include female offenders typically fail to examine possible sex differences in treatment outcome. Often it is not even possible to determine from project reports whether female subjects were included in a study. Many project reports simply make no mention of the sex of the subjects and the reader is left to assume, correctly or not, that they were male offenders.

•Small samples: Many conclusions about the value of programs are based on studies using samples which are much too small to warrant any firm conclusions.

•Program quality and integrity: The following statements from a report which claimed success for a project in which untrained probation officers provided group counselling to probationers illustrate the cavalier attitude that has too long characterized program planning:

> The probation officers assuming group counselling responsibilities had only the most elementary understanding of group work methods and techniques. We assumed, however, that they did have something to offer in working with groups, and we decided that . . . each officer would be permitted to develop his own operational techniques . . .
>
> (Faust, 1965)

•**Atheoretical:** The vast majority of programs are theoretically barren. Many programs appear to have developed in response to a "fad" rather than to a careful conceptualization of the female offender's problems. Programs for female offenders are typically conceived in a theoretical vacuum.

•**Program components:** Most researchers have relied on global evaluation of programs without attempting to ascertain the relative contribution of particular program components to determine what is essential, what is detrimental and what is merely extravagant. Unfortunately, there are not enough adequate studies to make a meta-analysis of programs possible.

•**Replication of failure:** We found no study which reported having examined the treatment history of female offenders, and we can only wonder whether, as they proceed through different segments of the correctional system, female offenders are involved in the same programs which have been tried with them in the past in unsuccessful rehabilitation efforts. Our analysis of vocational training services revealed that many institutional programs train offenders in those areas in which they already have been trained.

•**Criteria for success:** The problem of obtaining appropriate measures of program outcome is more difficult for female offenders than for male offenders (Palmer, 1978). This is particularly the case for juvenile female offenders, who are disproportionately represented among status offenders (Chesney-Lind, 1978; Landau, 1975). It is difficult to determine whether success in such cases can be judged in terms of the client's ability to evade further involvement with the criminal justice system when there are doubts about the justification for her involvement in it in the first place, and when the lack of further "offenses" might indicate, not changed behavior, but only changed status as a result of increasing age.

Relying exclusively on recidivism rates for both adolescent and adult female offenders tells only part of the story:

> The quality of life experienced by these women after discharge was very disappointing. . . . So many were leading marginal existences in terms of emotional, financial, and residential measures . . . . In strictly correctional terms, two thirds of those studied might be labelled "rehabilitated"; they had no further convictions. But about one half of these was barely making it on the streets (p. 325).
>
> (Lambert & Madden, 1976)

Informed Policy

Clearly there is a very limited body of research on program outcomes on which to base policy formation. Moreover, there are three glaring gaps in our knowledge which should have priority in research:

1. The literature on programs for female offenders is concerned almost exclusively with women in prisons. They comprise an extremely low percentage of female offenders and may not be representative of female offenders in general. The vast majority of female offenders are in community corrections or in local jails, but almost nothing is known about their characteristics or the programs they receive (if any) (Bowker, 1978). Particularly in Canada, the concern for services for women in prison has served to reduce the attention on juveniles and adult offenders in community settings.
2. Minority females are inordinately represented in the offender population. They have been selectively ignored in most research on correctional services (and in the provision of programs and services).
3. Attention has been fixed almost exclusively on *adult* female offenders; reports on services for young female offenders have been rare.

Although there has been very little adequate evaluation of correctional services for female offenders, there have been a sufficient number of well-controlled studies whose results suggest a number of general directions and emphases for policy development, program planning and service delivery.

In the first place, we would recommend that rather than basing program development for women on what is "in vogue," or on what is available for men, policy and planning should be based on an objective and realistic assessment of the characteristics, needs and circumstances of the offender. This has seldom been done.

Client Profiles

Our recommendations for correctional services for female offenders are derived from a profile of the female offender gleaned from a number of descriptive studies reported in the literature (e.g. Cloninger & Guze, 1973; Cowie, Cowie & Slater, 1968; Felice & Offord, 1971; Glick & Neto, 1977; Hendrix, 1972; PPWGO, 1970). The profile represents a very generalized picture because of the variety of settings in which those studies were conducted. Obviously, local assessment is required.

The most salient feature of the female offender population is the overrepresentation of women from minority groups: in the United States, blacks; in Canada, natives. The next most salient feature is that they are poor, undereducated, and lacking in marketable skills. Although many are single parents and heads of households, most are unemployed (or unemployable) welfare recipients lacking means to adequately support their dependent children or themselves. The majority of them have worked at some time in their lives, but usually not on a regular basis and typically in low-paying, unskilled, or semiskilled occupations.

A large number (fifty to seventy percent) have children; many have two or three. Fifty percent of their children are of preschool age, and the majority are under ten. Approximately thirty-five to sixty percent of the children were not in their mother's care at the time of her arrest. Although sixty percent of adult female offenders have been married at least once, only ten percent were actually living with their husband at the time of arrest. Husbands are rarely involved in child care or in providing financial support.

The majority of incarcerated women are under thirty years of age; the median age is about twenty-four to twenty-six. The majority have been involved in nonviolent crimes such as theft, fraud, embezzlement, or other property-related crimes, and in drug-related offenses.

Although some have university education (usually drug offenders), the majority have high school education or less. Their educational level is highly correlated with ethnic origin; white offenders are usually much better educated than either natives or blacks.

A substantial number of female offenders are drug and/or alcohol abusers. Approximately twenty percent have had previous commitments to mental hospitals; about seventeen percent have attempted suicide. Most of the offenders come from disunited and multiproblem families in which poverty, unemployment, desertion, alcoholism, drug addiction, and criminality in parents and siblings were common. Many were victims of both sexual and physical abuse in childhood and/or early adolescence; many in later adolescence and adulthood were living in abusive relationships with men on whom they were financially and emotionally dependent.

Finally, we must note that a characteristic of many female offenders is dependency—on welfare, alcohol, and men.

•**Individual assessment:** Although the foregoing profile provides a reasonably accurate general picture of the female offender population, program planners must base their decisions on assessment of local populations. In most situations they probably will face the problem of dealing with a diverse heterogeneous offender population. Continuing to pursue homogeneous goals for a heterogeneous population is likely to continue to be fruitless. Individualized assessment is required. This must include needs assessment from the perspective of the offender herself. Assessment should consider not only personality variables but also environmental and economic factors, which may be stronger determinants of the offender's illegal behavior.

•**Classification:** Also required is an adequate classification scheme to facilitate program planning and service delivery. Unfortunately, there is as yet very little research that would enable us to determine on what basis differential security or programming might best be provided. Partly because of the small number of female offenders, little interest has been shown in developing classification criteria for them (Datesman, Scarpitti & Stephenson, 1975; Widom, 1978). The development of such criteria may be fostered by recent factor-analytic studies of female offenders (Pierce, Asarnow & Ross, 1978) and recent research on the different levels of supervision required for different types of offenders (Andrews & Kiessling, 1980; Bonta & Motiuk, 1985). In many jurisdictions which provide only one centralized institution for women, female offenders are not even classified by geography. Their sex is the only factor that is usually considered in classification.

More refined classification of offenders is required not only at the institution level; it is required throughout the correctional system in such a way that a woman's needs for security, supervision, and programming can be accommodated such that they receive only the minimum level of intervention, control, and custody they require.

However, classification is likely to be only an academic exercise or a paper-chase if the variety of facilities and services appropriate to the classificatory criteria are not forthcoming.

Diversified Service

DeConstanzo & Valente (1984) have recently presented a model for a correctional system for female offenders. Essentially, they recommend the provision of a continuum of correctional options, including not only the three standard components (probation/prison/parole) but many other options: restitution (including fines and community service orders); probation with intensive services provided by a specially trained probation officer or ancillary staff; probation with the offender confined to her home except for special program involvement; probation with required participation at a co-ed community attendance center (for training, etc.); probation while living in supervised housing; probation while residing in a community residential correctional center (co-ed, or single sex with shared program facilities); earned release with surveillance; and postinstitutional community residential centers (various kinds of halfway houses with different levels of security and with or without community access).

Program Sharing

We suggest that women be enabled to share programs and services available to male offenders (when they are appropriate to their needs) and we recommend that, in the case of institutionalized offenders, this be provided not only through co-correctional establishments, but, perhaps preferably, through "cooperative" programs in which services are shared but housing is separate.

In terms of their socioeconomic circumstances and their needs for services and programs, female offenders appear to have more in common with other women, particularly disadvantaged women, than they do with male offenders. Accordingly, more emphasis should be placed on sharing programs with agencies which provide services for other women. The sharing of services requires the sharing of resources; it is necessary to ensure that the other agencies benefit from such sharing.

The success or failure of any institutional program or service will depend to a great extent on the kinds and extent of supports offered to the woman after she is released.

Correctional Staff

The Achilles heel of any correctional service is its staff. Effective programming requires effective staff members; so does effective program planning. The literature on female offenders seldom discusses this matter save to recommend, with some justification, an increase in the representation of female staff in corrections (e.g. Brodsky, 1974; Schoonmaker & Brooks, 1975; Velimesis, 1975). Such increases need to be made not only at the line-staff level, but at the policy and planning level and in management.

Increasing the number of female staff is not sufficient. Increase in their quality is also required. Staff should be selected who are nonsexist in their attitudes, interpersonally sensitive, and empathetic, but able to be directive in their supervision and consistent in enforcing rules and regulations. They must be models of anticriminal attitudes and behavior and of prosocial problem-solving skills (Andrews & Kiessling, 1980; Ross & Fabiano, 1985).

Program Development

All Things to All People

It is hardly likely that correctional agencies will have the resources to provide all of the facilities and services which have been recommended in the literature and which seem to be required by the multiproblem characteristic of many female offenders. On the other hand, it is unrealistic, though not uncommon, to expect major change from minor, weak, or superficial programs. "Puny interventions" will not work. It is by no means a simple matter for an offender to go straight, or to remain straight (Birkenmayer, 1984).

Accordingly, one must ask, given the acknowledged limits of the available data on program effectiveness, how correctional agencies might best be advised to invest their resources. In our view, the research literature gives rather clear guidelines as to the general areas in which emphasis should be placed in the allocation of resources. In general, we suggest that the primary objective for program planning should be the provision of service and program opportunities and supports which will maximize the likelihood that female offenders will develop social competence and the ability to become economically self-sufficient. This suggestion is based on several assumptions:

1. The model which has most commonly guided the development of programs for female offenders has been the medical or disease model. The lack of evidence of the success of programs derived from an understanding of female crime in terms of psychopathology raises doubts about a disease model of female criminality. Explanations of female criminality in terms of presumed anatomical or physiological deficiencies, have, in addition to their other shortcomings, failed to stimulate effective treatment programs.

In contrast, we recommend a social competence model which is based on a view of criminal behavior in terms of social and economic factors and takes an educational/developmental approach rather than a therapeutic approach to offender rehabilitation (Chapman, 1980; Ross & Fabiano, 1985). We assume that many female offenders enter the correctional system and remain in it because they lack the skills to make it elsewhere.

> Why are the more progressive correctional systems so willing to spend money on casework and "therapy" to help women develop empathy, maturity, unselfishness, warmth and effect and so little to help provide the skills and create the conditions under which these personal attributes can flower?
>
> (Velimesis, 1981)

2. Although the model we propose focuses on the offender and on offender change, it also assumes that offender change is likely to be maintained only if (a) the situational factors which have influenced her criminal behavior are changed (this is usually an unlikely eventuality), or (b) the offender acquires skills which allow her to cope with these situational factors or enable her to change her situation. She will also require support to deal with situational pressures such as housing, family relations, finances, and child care.

3. Multifaceted programs are required. There are no simple, patent remedies; no panaceas. Programs must be comprehensive; not unlike offenders, they must be complex. Most offenders are

likely to have multiple problems. No single program modality is likely to be effective with *all* of these problems.

4. An adequate correctional response to the rehabilitative needs of many female offenders must include an alcohol or drug abuse program. Such programs must be designed specifically for females. Programs based on social learning principles which include training in cognitive and social skills and in problem-solving may have the greatest potential in dealing with substance abuse (Ross & Lightfoot, 1985).

5. Programs should target those factors which are most correlated with continued illegal behavior. The limited research on persistent criminal behavior in females points to the importance of two factors: employment skills and social skills.

Employment

Although no adequate evaluation studies of vocational programs for female offenders have been conducted, analyses of available programs makes it clear that to be effective a program will have to satisfy a number of requirements:

1. An adequate amount, intensity and quality of training must be provided. It is unrealistic to expect a few weeks of training to overcome years of dependency, low self-esteem . . . "a limited amount of training is worse than none at all, because it increases expectation but not opportunity" (Sorensen, 1981).

2. Training should be offered in work that is relevant to the job market, and flexibility must be provided to accord with changes in that market.

3. Training must focus on jobs which have the potential to earn the women a salary sufficient to attain economic independence. Welfare and/or criminal activity may yield a better living than working at minimum-wage jobs. Innovation is required, such as has been demonstrated in the development of courses in some women's prisons in optics, microfilm processing, appliance repair, reprographics, braille, meat cutting, commercial art, printing, electronics, and waste water management. It also requires ongoing study of the labor market and flexibility to accord with changes in that market.

4. Training must be in fields in which the women show an

interest; their views must be determined and must be considered in program planning. This is seldom done.

5. At least as much effort must be focused on the offender's *motivation* for training as on the selection of training content. The provision of high-interest courses in fields with potential for adequate salaries is important, but so too are good trainers. The use of behavioral contracting, mutual agreement programs, and vouchers may also enhance offender motivation, participation, and persistence.

6. The correctional agency considering the provision of training for nontraditional jobs must first determine whether the potential trainees wish to assume such a new role, understand the consequences of such a change, and have the personal strengths and skills which will allow them to adjust to such a change. As Wheeler (1978) noted, "We should let our women say something about where they are and where they want to be and where they want to go."

It should be noted that surveys have indicated that although a significant number of offenders desire nontraditional training, the majority desire programming in those areas of work traditionally accessible to the female population at large.

7. In programming for vocational training and job placement it is essential that consideration be given to the implications of parental responsibility. Children can make enormous demands on the offender's time, emotional resources, and income. The demands of maintaining small children, usually as a single parent, may not be compatible with the intensive training and commitment required for entry into nontraditional jobs or other high-paying jobs. Support services, including day care, must be considered as part of employment planning.

8. Whereas gainful employment after release should be the goal of industrial and vocational programs in prisons, the other benefits of meaningful employment and training in prisons should not be overlooked:

> Look, our getting into "industries" may not seem like any big deal. But that pay makes a helluva difference when you hit the streets, and it sure can take off the pressure to "hustle" in here. But it's not just the pay, it's a time during the day when you're treated like a human being, not an inmate.
>
> (quoted in Hargrove & Faucett, 1978)

Service Delivery

Vocational training for female offenders requires innovation in service delivery. "In-house" training may be essential in some facilities and with particular inmates, but the cost of equipment and personnel is often very high, and flexibility in terms of accommodation to a changing job market may be prohibited with in-house programs. Many institutions (for either males or females) continue to provide training in jobs which are no longer in demand and do so with out-of-date equipment because the cost of "refitting" is more than meager correctional budgets can afford.

Many jurisdictions have made much more progress in establishing the necessary variety and quality of occupational training by other service delivery modes. Some institutions have arranged to share facilities, trainers, and budgets with institutions for male offenders; some involve offenders in programs which are provided for women in the community; some use facilities in local colleges and trade schools; some have established programs in which industries provide training (and, later, jobs) either in the community or the institution; some institutions provide facilities and employees (inmates) for industries which, in return, provide training for the offenders (in some cases, industry supplies the equipment, material, and trainers).

Training must not be limited to institutionalized offenders. Innovative and impressive programs have typically been community-based and have involved offenders on work-release, probation, parole, and (long-term) halfway houses.

Multifaceted Programs

Motivating, training, and placing female offenders in worthwhile jobs is by no means a simple task. Our analysis of the research literature suggests that success will probably require a multifaceted approach involving not only quality training but also most of the following components:

•**Occupational awareness/vocational counselling:** The offenders must be helped to understand and appreciate which vocational areas are likely to provide adequate employment for them and which are realistic and appropriate to their abilities, personality, interest, motivation, and personal circumstances. Information needs to be provided about what kinds of occupations exist, what benefits and disadvantages they yield, and what training, personal qualities, and certification are required. Many offenders need counselling about their limited job aspirations; others about their unrealistic expectations.

•**Job-readiness training:** Many female offenders need training in job search procedures—how to look for a job and how to interview for the job. Many have low self-esteem and lack both social skills and basic work skills. They require programs for these problems if they are realistically to be expected to obtain and retain jobs.

Job readiness training is particularly required for those who pursue nontraditional vocations. They must learn how to respond to resistance from employers and peers, isolation, ridicule, and harassment. They may also need pretraining in basic skills which many women lack and most men acquire in growing up: applied math, motor maintenance, basic mechanics, use of tools, etc.

An important aspect of job-readiness training is counselling on child care. Also required is counselling on money management and health.

•**Job development and placement:** Opportunities for jobs are by no means plentiful for female offenders. An adequate employment program must not only exert considerable efforts in teaching offenders how to search for jobs, but also must be aggressive, persistent and innovative in efforts to help them find jobs and in placing offenders in them. Failure to do so, particularly in a time of high unemployment, will likely mean the vocational program is for naught. It will also lead to further discouragement (and possibly to reactive antisocial behavior) for offenders whose expectations have been enhanced by vocational training.

•**Employer preparation:** Job development entails not only knocking on doors of prospective employers but also preparing them in terms of what benefits and problems to expect in hiring a female offender and how best to respond to these problems. Providing support for the employer (particularly encouragement and reinforcement) may be just as valuable as providing support for the offender. The use of explicit employment contingency contracts with the offender may be particularly helpful in reassuring both parties that appropriate action (positive or negative) will be taken depending on whether the offender performs well or poorly.

•**Follow-up services:** The probability that an offender will maintain a job may be contingent on the availability of support services available to her. Counselling and child care services may be essential, particularly through the first few months of employment. Counselling may be required particularly on matters such as health, money management, and relationships with spouses, coworkers, and employers.

Specific descriptions of exemplary employment services which offer each of these program components have been provided by Chapman (1980); Contact (1978); Hargrove & Faucett (1978); Milton et al. (1976, 1977); North (1975); and Spencer & Berecochea, (1972). Although these programs have not been rigorously evaluated, the impressive results of Walter & Mills' (1980) behavioral employment intervention program indicate the value of such multifaceted approaches. This methodologically sound program dramatically reduced delinquent behavior in female (and male) delinquents by helping them obtain jobs, recruiting and training employers, using employment contingency contracts with the offenders, and reinforcing both the offender's proemployment behaviors and the employer's commitment.

Social Competence

Whereas vocational training may be valuable, even essential for many female offenders, it must be noted that in spite of market-relevant and quality training, in a time of massive unemployment, it may not be possible for many female offenders to obtain jobs. Moreover, for some offenders, because of their behavior problems, their limited intellectual or social skills, or their poor motivation or because of situational demands (particularly child care), employment in an adequately paying job may simply not be a realistic possibility. Vocational training may not fulfill the rehabilitative requirements for many offenders who require not jobs but shelter and support; not vocational training, but training in life skills, social skills, and coping skills.

Many need training in such essential skills as budgeting, banking, obtaining and discharging credit, purchasing, obtaining housing, household management, how to use community resources, medical and dental health, nutrition, birth control, legal rights and procedures (including divorce, separation, and marital rights) dealing with child abuse, child care, and child welfare.

In short, they need training in survival skills, in self-management skills, in independent living skills (Chapman, 1980). They need to learn how to control their lives; to learn that they can do things for themselves without depending on others. Since many will become single heads of households, they need to recognize their responsibilities to themselves and their children and how best to handle them. They need to learn how to cope with public agencies, with money, with independence, and with or without men.

Time to Think

Many female offenders also need training in cognitive skills. Teaching offenders how to *think* may be at least as important as teaching them how to behave (Ross & Fabiano, 1985).

Programs are required which would foster the development of the offender's reasoning skills and her social comprehension. She needs to learn how to think logically, objectively and rationally. She needs to learn to stop, think, and analyze consequences before taking action; to formulate plans and to more adequately conceptualize the means whereby she might satisfy her needs. Many need to be taught how to analyze interpersonal problems, how to understand other people's values, behavior, and feelings; how to recognize how their own behavior affects other people and why they respond to them as they do. They need to learn how to think of alternative, prosocial ways of reacting to interpersonal conflicts.

A variety of programs and techniques have been developed to achieve such goals. They include role-playing and modelling, rational self-analysis, self-control training, means-end reasoning, critical thinking, values education, and a variety of cognitive restructuring techniques (Ross & Fabiano, 1985).

Offenders may particularly benefit from training in interpersonal cognitive problem-solving, which can enhance their ability to recognize and analyze interpersonal problems, lead them to consider the consequences of their behavior, teach them to consider alternative courses of action, and help them to understand the behavior thoughts and feelings of other people.

Final Word

The design, management, and control of women's prisons are beyond the scope of this review, but it is essential that we reiterate the many recommendations that have been made about the necessity of ensuring that women should have the option of being housed in institutions near their home community, not only to maintain their ties with their children, but to increase their accessibility to training and employment services in the community to which they will be released.

We must add that there are many women who should not be imprisoned at all. Such women could well be accommodated without threat to society in facilities and services such as those recommended by DeConstanzo & Valente (1984) . . . if those facilities and services were available.

Whereas we are recommending more use of community services, we do so with the proviso that care is taken to ensure that these services are relevant to the offender's needs and are of sufficient quality to be of help. The fact that services exist in the community is no guarantee that they will be worthwhile. Too often, community programs for female offenders have provided only alterations in correctional geography; the community has been only a new place for old techniques.

Bibliography

Adams, S. *Assessment of the psychiatric treatment program: Second interim report.* Research Report No. 15, California Youth Authority, 1959.

________. *Development of a program research service in probation.* Los Angeles County Probation Department, Research Report Number 27, Los Angeles, 1966.

________. *Effectiveness of the Youth Authority Special Treatment Program: First interim report.* Research Report No. 5, California Youth Authority, 1959.

Adams, S.G. *The female offender: A statistical perspective.* Canada: Ministry of the Solicitor General, 1978.

Adler, A. Rehabilitative programs for women. In *Rehabilitation what part of corrections?,* ed. B. Broadshaw and P.J. Ecks. Research Service Division Institute of Urban Studies, Arlington, 1977.

Adler, F. *Sisters in crime.* New York: McGraw-Hill, 1975.

________, and R.J. Simon. eds. *The criminology of deviant women.* Boston: Houghton Mifflin, 1979.

Alexander, J.F., C. Barton, R.S. Schiaro and B.V. Parsons. Systems-behavioral intervention with families of delinquents: Therapist characteristics and family behavior and outcome. *Journal of Consulting and Clinical Psychology* **44** (1976): 656–664.

________, and R.J. Parsons. Short-term behavioral intervention with delinquent families: Impact on family process and recidivism. *Journal of Abnormal Psychology* **81** (1973): 219–225.

Alexander, R.N. The effects of individual and group consequences on school attendance and curfew violations with pre-delinquent adolescents. *Journal of Applied Behavior Analysis* **9** (1976): 221–226.

American Bar Association. *Community programs for women offenders: Cost and economic considerations.* Washington, D.C.: 1975.

________. *Female offenders: Problems and programs.* Washington, D.C.: Female Offender Resource Center, 1976.

Anderson, D.C. Co-corrections. *Corrections Magazine,* **7** (Sept. 1978): 31–41.

Anderson, E. Ringe. A new maximum-security prison for young men and women in Denmark. In *Confinement in maximum custody,* ed. D. Wood and K. Schoen. Toronto: D.C. Heath, 1981, 159–173.

Andrews, D.A., J. Bonta, L. Motiuk, and D. Robinson. *Some psychometrics of practical risk/needs assessments.* Paper presented at the Annual Meeting of the American Psychological Association, Toronto, 1984.

________, and J.J. Kiessling. Program structure and effective correctional practices. In *Effective correctional treatment,* ed. R.R. Ross and P. Gendreau. Toronto: Butterworth, 1980.

Arditi, R.R., and F. Goldberg. Sexual segregation of American prisons. *Mental Health Digest* **5**, no. 9 (1973): 18–26.

________, F. Goldberg, M. Hartle, J.H. Peters, and W.R. Phelps. The sexual segregation of American prisons. *The Yale Law Journal* **82** (1973): 1229–1273.

Arnold, J.E., A.G. Levine, and G.R. Patterson. Changes in sibling behavior following family intervention. *Journal of Consulting and Clinical Psychology* **5** (1975): 683–688.

Arter, R.M. *New England intervention programs: Final report for the period July 1, 1975–April 30, 1977.* New York: Research and Action, Inc., 1977.

Bahna, G., and N.B. Gordon. Rehabilitation experiences of women ex-addicts in methadone treatment. *The International Journal of the Addictions* **13**, no. 4 (1978): 639–655.

Bahr, S.J. Family determinants and effects of deviance. In *Contemporary theories about the family: Research-based theories,* Vol. 1, ed. W.R. Burr, R. Hill, F.I. Nye, and I.L. Reiss. New York: Free Press, 1979.

Bailey, K.G. Audiotape self-confrontation in group psychotherapy. *Psychological Reports* **27** (1970): 439–444.

Barkwell, L.J. Differential treatment on probation: An evaluation study.

In *Effective correctional treatment*, ed. R.R. Ross and P. Gendreau. Toronto: Butterworth, 1980.

Bateman, N.I., and D.M. Petersen. Factors related to outcome of treatment for hospitalized white male and female alcoholics. *Journal of Drug Issues* **2** (1972): 66–74.

Baunach, P.J. You can't be a mother and be in prison . . . can you? Impacts on the mother-child separation. In *The criminal justice system and women,* ed. B.R. Price and W.J. Sokoloff. New York: Clark Boardman, 1982.

________, and T.D. Murton. Women in prison—an awakening minority. *Crime and Corrections* **1**, no. 2 (1973): 4–12.

Beckman, L.J. Women alcoholics: A review of social and psychological studies. *Journal of Studies on Alcohol* **36** (1975): 797–824.

Bedford, A. Women and parole. *British Journal of Criminology* **14** (1974): 106–117.

Belfer, M.L., R.I. Shader, M. Carroll, and J.S. Harmantz. Alcoholism in women. *Archives of General Psychiatry* **25** (1971): 540–544.

Bell, R. *Correctional education programs for inmates.* Lehigh University, School of Education, 1977.

Berzins, L., and S. Cooper. Political economy of correctional planning for women—The case of the bankrupt bureaucracy. *Canadian Journal of Criminology* **24**, no. 4 (1982): 399–416.

Birkenmayer, A.C. Personal communication, 1984.

________, M. Polonoski, S. Pirs, and D. McLaren. *A preliminary evaluation of the group home programme.* Ontario: Ministry of Correctional Services, 1975.

Bohme, K., H. Buhe, and H. Schluturo. Social therapy for women. *International Summaries* **2** (1978).

Bonta, J. and L. Motiuk. The utilization of an interview based classification instrument in correctional half-way houses. *Criminal Justice and Behavior,* 1985 (in press).

Bowker, L.H. *Women, crime, and the criminal justice system.* Lexington, Mass.: D.C. Heath, 1978.

Bradshaw, B., and P.J. Ecks. *Rehabilitation what part of corrections?,* Research Service Division Institute of Urban Studies, Arlington, 1977.

Braukman, C.J., and D.L. Fixsen. Behavior modification with delinquents. In *Progress in behavior modification,* Vol. 1, ed. M. Hersen. New York: Academic Press, 1975.

Brodsky, A.M. Planning for the female offender – Directions for the future. *Criminal Justice and Behavior* **1**, no. 4 (1974), 392–400.

Buckles, D.A. and M.A. Fazia. Child care for mothers in prison. In *Social work practice and social justice,* ed. B. Ross and C. Cheremain. New York: National Association of Social Workers, 1973.

Buehler, R.E., G.R. Patterson, and J.M. Furniss. The reinforcement of behavior in institutional settings. *Behavior Research and Therapy* **4** (1966), 157–167.

Burkhart, K.W. *Women in prison.* New York: Doubleday, 1973.

Byles, J.A., and A. Maurice. The juvenile services project: An experiment in delinquency control. *Canadian Journal of Criminology* **21**, no. 2 (1979), 155–165.

Carkhuff, R.R. *The development of human resources.* New York: Holt, Rinehart & Winston, 1971.

Chandler, M.J. Egocentrism and antisocial behavior. In *Effective correctional treatment,* ed. R.R. Ross and P. Gendreau. Toronto: Butterworth, 1980.

Chapman, J.R. *Economic realities and the female offender.* Toronto: Lexington Books, 1980.

________. *Employment preparation for female offenders: An overview.* Paper presented at the Annual Meeting of the American Correctional Association, Philadelphia, Pennsylvania, August 21, 1979.

Cherkas, M.S. Synanon foundation – A radical approach to the problem of addiction. *American Journal of Psychiatry* **121** (1965), 1065–1068.

Chesney-Lind, M. Young women in the arms of the law. In *Women, crime and the criminal justice system,* by L.H. Bowker. Lexington, Mass.: D.C. Heath, 1978.

Christenson, S.J. and A.Q. Swanson. Women and drug use: An annotated bibliography. *Journal of Psychedelic Drugs* **6**, no. 4 (1974), 371–413.

Cloninger, C.R., and S.B. Guze. Psychiatric illness in the families of female criminals: A study of 288 first degree relatives. *British Journal of Psychiatry* **122** (1973), 697–703.

Coleman, B.I. Helping women addicts in New York City. *International Journal of Offender Therapy & Comparative Criminology* **18**, no. 1 (1974), 82–85.

Collingwood, T.R., A. Douds, and H. Williams. Juvenile diversion: The Dallas Police Department Youth Services Program. *Federal Probation* **40**, no. 3 (1976): 23–27.

Contact, Inc. *Woman offender.* Lincoln, Neb., 1978.

Cook, P.J. The correctional carrot: Better jobs for parolees. *Policy Analysis* **I** (1975): 11–51.

Copeman, C.D., and P.L. Shaw. Effects of contingent management of addicts expecting commitment to a community based treatment program. *British Journal of Addiction* **71**, no. 2 (1976): 187–191.

Cowie, J., V. Cowie, and E. Slater. *Delinquency in girls.* London: Heineman, 1968.

Cox, G.B., S.J. Carmichael, and C. Dightman. An evaluation of a community-based diagnostic program for juvenile offenders. *Juvenile Justice* (August 1977): 33–41.

Crites, L., ed. *The female offender.* Lexington, Mass.: D.C. Heath, 1976.

Cunningham, G. Supervision of the female offender. *Federal Probation* **27**, no. 4 (1963): 12–16.

Curlee, J. Alcoholic women: Some considerations for further research. *Bulletin of the Menninger Clinic* **31** (1967): 154–163.

Cuskey, W.R., and R.B. Wathey. *Female addiction.* Toronto: Lexington Books, 1980.

Datesman, S.K., F.R. Scarpitti, and R.M. Stephenson. Female delinquency: An application of self and opportunity theories. *Journal of Research in Crime and Delinquency* (1975): 107–123.

Davidson, W.S., and E. Seidman. Studies of behavior modification in juvenile delinquency: A review, methodological critique, and social perspective. *Psychological Bulletin* **81** (1974): 998–1011.

Davis, H.F. *Variables associated with recovery in male and female alcoholics following hospitalization.* Doctoral dissertation, Texas Technological College, 1966.

DeConstanzo, E.T., and J. Valente. Designing a correction continuum for female offenders: One state's experience. *The Prison Journal* **64**, no. 1 (Spring/Summer 1984).

DeLeon, G., S. Holland, and M.S. Rosenthal. Phoenix House. Criminal activity of dropouts. *Journal of the American Medical Association* (1972): 222, 686–689.

———, and N. Jainchill. Male and female drug abusers: Social and psychological status two years after treatment in a therapeutic community. *American Journal of Drug and Alcohol Abuse* **8**, no. 4 (1982).

———, A. Skodol, and M.S. Rosenthal. Phoenix House. *Archives of General Psychiatry* **28** (1973): 131–135.

Densen-Gerber, J., and D. Drassner. Odyssey House: A structural model for the successful employment and re-entry of the ex-drug abuser. *Journal of Drug Issues* **4** (1974): 414–427.

DeVault, B. Women parolees. *Crime and Delinquency* **11** (1965): 272–282.

Duguid, S. Moral development, justice and democracy in the prison. *Canadian Journal of Criminology* **23**, no. 2 (1981): 147–162.

Duncan, D.F. Verbal behavior in a detention home. *Corrective and Social Psychiatry and Journal of Behavior Technology Method and Therapy* **18** (1972): 22–31.

Elder, P.D. House for ex-Borstal girls: An exploratory project. *British Journal of Criminology* **12**, no. 4 (1972): 357–374.

Elliot, D.S., and H.L. Voss. *Delinquency and dropout.* Lexington, Mass.: Lexington Books, 1974.

Emory, R.E., and D. Marholin II. An applied behavior analysis of delinquency: The irrelevancy of relevant behavior. *American Psychologist* **32** (1977): 860–873.

Eyeberg, S., and S.M. Johnson. Multiple assessment of behavior modification with families: Effects of contingency contracting and order of treated persons. *Journal of Consulting and Clinical Psychology* **42** (1974): 594–606.

Faily, A., and G. A. Roundtree. Study of aggression and rule violations in a female prison population. *Journal of Offender Counseling, Services & Rehabilitation* **4**, no. 1 (1979): 81–87.

Faust, F.L. Group counseling with juveniles by staff without professional training in group work. *Crime and Delinquency* **11**, no. 4 (1965): 349–354.

Feinman, C. Sex-role stereotypes and justice for women. *Crime and Delinquency,* (January 1979): 87–94.

Felice, M., and D.R. Offord. Girl delinquency: A review. *Corrective Psychiatry and Journal of Social Therapy* **17**, no. 2 (1971): 18–33.

Fine, J. Exploratory study to measure the post release effectiveness of work-training release programs. *Offender Rehabilitation* **2** (1978): 215–224.

Fixsen, D., E. Phillips, and M. Wolf. Achievement Place: Experiments in self-government with pre-delinquents. *Journal of Applied Behavior Analysis* **6** (1973): 31–47.

Fo, W.S., and C.R. O'Donnell. The buddy system: Effect of community intervention on delinquent offences. *Behavior Therapy* **6** (1975): 522–524.

_______, and _______. The buddy system: Relationship and contingency conditions in a community intervention program for youth with nonprofessionals as behavior change agents. *Journal of Consulting and Clinical Psychology* **42**, no. 2 (1974): 163–169.

Footes, L.E. Effect of achievement motivation training on women prisoners. *Criminal Justice and Behavior* **1**, no. 2 (June 1974): 131–138.

Fox, V., and M.A. Smith. Evaluation of a chemo-psychotherapeutic program for the rehabilitation of alcoholics: Observations over a two-year period. *Quarterly Journal of Studies on Alcohol* **20** (1959): 767–780.

Ganter, G. *Teen-Aid, Inc. Update report.* Pennsylvania Governor's Justice Commission, 1976.

Ganzer, V.J., and I.G. Sarason. Variables associated with recidivism among juvenile delinquents. *Journal of Consulting and Clinical Psychology* **40** (1973): 1–5.

Garrell-Michaud, V. *Manchester (N.H.) YWCA female intervention project evaluation.* New Hampshire Governor's Commission on Crime and Delinquency (October 1979): 463–489.

Gendreau, P., D. Burke, and B.A. Grant. A second evaluation of the Rideau Inmate Volunteer Program. *Canadian Journal of Criminology* **22** (1980): 66–77.

Gibbs, C. The effect of imprisonment of women upon their children. *British Journal of Criminology* **11**, no. 2 (1971): 113–130.

Gibson, H. Women's prisons: Laboratories for penal reform. *Wisconsin Law Review* (1973): 210–233.

_______. Women's prisons: Laboratories for penal reform. In *The female offender,* ed. L. Crites. Toronto: D.C. Heath, 1976.

Glasser, W. *Reality therapy: A new approach to psychiatry.* New York: Harper Colophon Books, 1965.

Glick, R.M., and V.V. Neto. *National study of women's correctional programs.* Washington, D.C.: National Institute of Law Enforcement and Criminal Justice, 1977.

Goldberg, M. Confrontation groups in a girls' approved school. *British Journal of Criminology* (April 1974): 132–138.

Goldstein, A.P., M. Sherman, N.J. Gershaw, R.P. Sprafkin, and B. Gluck. Training aggressive adolescents in prosocial behavior. *Journal of Youth and Adolescence* **7**, no. 1 (1978).

Goodman, N., E. Maloney, and J. Davis. Borstal girls eight years after release. In *Further studies of female offenders.* Home Office Research Study No. 33. London: H.M.S.O., 1976.

Greening, B. Prison for moms and kids. *Youth Authority Quarterly* **31** (1978): 25–30.

Haft, M.G. Women in prison: Discriminatory practices and some solutions. *Clearinghouse Review* **8** (1974): 1–6.

Handler, E. Residential treatment programs for juvenile delinquents. *Social Work* **20** (1975): 217–222.

Hankinson, I. Probation research—its implication for the service. *Social Work Today* **10**, no. 36 (1979): 17–18.

Hargrove, A.H., and J.E. Faucett. *Women offenders in non-traditional work.* Washington, D.C.: Wider Opportunities for Women, 1978.

Hendrix, O. *A study in neglect: A report on women's prisons.* New York: Women's Prison Association, 1972.

Hopson, J. and H. Rosenfeld. PMS: Puzzling monthly symptoms. *Psychology Today* (August 1984): 36–38.

Hovatter, D. *Adventure trails.* Dallas, Tex.: Personnel Communication, 1979.

Hudson, J. Experimental study of parole supervision of juvenile and social service utilization. *IOWA Journal of Social Work* **4** (1976, Special Issue): 80–89.

Hunt, G.M., and N.H. Azrin. A community-reinforcement approach to alcoholism. *Behavior Research and Therapy* **11** (1973): 91–104.

Inciardi, J.A., and D.C. Chambers. Unreported criminal involvement of narcotics addicts. *Journal of Drug Issues* **2** (1972): 56–64.

Irish, J.F. *Probation and recidivism.* New York: Nassau County Probation Department.

James, I.P., and P.T. d'Orban. Patterns of delinquency among British heroin addicts. *Bulletin on Narcotics* **22** (1970): 13–19.

James, J., C. Gosho, and R.W. Wohl. The relationship between female criminality and drug use. *The International Journal of the Addictions* **14**, no. 2 (1979): 215–229.

James, S.R., F. Oxborn, and E.R. Oetling. Treatment for delinquent girls: The adolescent self-concept group. *Community Mental Health Journal* **3** (1967): 377–381.

Jesness, C., T. Allison, P. McCormick, R. Wedge, and M. Young. *An evaluation of the effectiveness of contingency contracting with delinquents.* Sacramento: California Department of the Youth Authority, 1975.

Johnson, D.C., R.W. Shearon, and G.M. Britton. Correctional education and recidivism in a women's correctional center. *Adult Education* **24**, no. 2 (1974): 121–129.

Johnson, T.F. The results of family therapy with juvenile offenders. *Juvenile Justice* (November 1977): 29–33.

Jones, M. *Maturation of the therapeutic community.* New York: Behavioral Science Publications, 1976.

Kasowski, E.M. *Follow-up appraisal of process and chance in a group home treatment program for disturbed adolescent girls.* Ph.D. dissertation, 1976.

Kaubin, B.J. Sexism shades the lives and treatment of female addicts. *Contemporary Drug Problems* **3** (1974): 471–484.

Kennedy, D.J. The Rideau Alcohol Program: A multi-disciplinary approach to alcohol related problems of incarcerated offenders. *Canadian Journal of Criminology* **22** (1980): 428–442.

Kent, R.N., and K.D. O'Leary. A controlled evaluation of behavior modification with conduct problem children. *Journal of Consulting and Clinical Psychology* **44** (1976): 586–596.

Ketterling, M.E. Rehabilitating women in jail. *Journal of Rehabilitation* **36** (1970): 36–38.

Kirkstra, C. *Parole outcome of female felony offenders from the Detroit House of Corrections.* Michigan Dept. of Corrections, 1967.

Klein, D. The etiology of female crime: A review of the literature. *Issues in Criminology* **8**, no. 2 (1973): 3–30.

Kloss, J.D. The impact of comprehensive community treatment: An asessment of the Complex Offender Project. *Offender Rehabilitation* **3**, no. 1 (1978): 81–108.

———. *Success and failure in the evaluation of behavioral community treatment.* Wisconsin: Mendota Mental Health Institute, 1980.

Knox, P.H. *Efficacy of assertive training in changing locus of control.* Ph.D. dissertation, Arizona State University, 1976.

Kohlberg, L., P. Scharf, and J. Hickey. The justice structure of the prison: a theory and an intervention. *Prison Journal* **51** (1971): 3–14.

Lambert, L.R. and P.B. Madden. The adult female offender: The road from institution to community life. *Canadian Journal of Criminology and Corrections* **18**, no. 4 (1976): 319–331.

———, and ———. *Vanier Centre Research.* Toronto: Ministry of Correctional Services, 1975.

Lampkin, A.C., and G.G. Taylor. *Second year Santa Clara County day care center evaluation.* San Jose, Calif.: American Justice Institute Research Unit, 1973.

Landau, B. The adolescent female offender: Our dilemma. *Canadian Journal of Criminology and Corrections* **17**, no. 2 (1975): 146–153.

Lee, R., and N.M. Haynes. Project CREST and the dual-treatment approach to delinquency: Methods and research summarized. In *Effective Correctional Treatment*, ed. R.R. Ross and P. Gendreau. Toronto, Butterworth, 1980.

Lerman, P., C. Lerman, D.T. Dickson, and B. Lagay. *New Jersey Training School for Girls: A study of alternatives.* Washington, D.C.: Law Enforcement Assistance Administration, 1974.

Levy, B. Art therapy in a women's correctional facility. *Art Psychotherapy* **5**, no. 3 (1978): 157–166.

Levy, S., and K. Doyle. Attitudes of female drug users. *Journal of Drug Issues* **4**, no. 4 (1974): 428–434.

Litt, I.F., and M.I. Cohen. Persons, adolescents and the right to quality medical care: The time is now. *American Journal of Public Health* **64** (1974): 894–897.

Lowe, P., and C. Stewart. Women in prison. In *Developments in social skills training,* ed. S. Spence and B. Shepherd. New York: Academic Press, 1983.

McCarthy, B.R. *Easy time: Female inmates on temporary release.* Toronto: D.C. Heath, 1979.

________. Inmate mothers – The problems of separation and reintegration. *Journal of Offender Counseling, Services and Rehabilitation* **4** (1980): 199–212.

McCombs, D., J. Filipczak, R.M. Friedman, and J.S. Wodarski. Long-term follow-up of behavior modification with high-risk adolescents. *Criminal Justice and Behavior* **5**, no. 1 (1978): 21–34.

McCord, J. *Correctional group counseling: An evaluation.* Paper presented at the National Conference on Criminal Justice Evaluation, 1977.

________. Some child-rearing antecedents of criminal behavior in adult men. *Journal of Personality and Social Psychology* **37** (1979): 1477–86.

McGowan, B.G., and K.L. Blumenthal. Children or women prisoners: A forgotten minority. *The female offender*, ed. L. Crites. Lexington Books, 1976.

________, and ________. *Why punish the children: A study of women prisoners.* Hackensack, N.J.: National Council on Crime and Delinquency, 1978.

McManus, J.E. Proctor program for detention of delinquent girls. *Child Welfare* **55**, no. 5 (1976): 345–352.

Mandel, L., J. Schulman, and R. Monteiro. A feminist approach for the treatment of drug-abusing women in a coed therapeutic community. *The International Journal of the Addictions* **14**, no. 5 (1979): 589–597.

Mandel, N.G., and H. B. Vinnes. *Effects of short-term group psychotherapy on the intra-institutional behavior of female felons.* Minnesota: Department of Corrections, 1968.

Marholin, D., II, A. J. Plienis, S.D. Harris, and B. L. Harholin. Mobilization of the community through a behavioral approach: A school program for adjudicated females. *Criminal Justice and Behavior* **2**, no. 2 (1975): 130–145.

Markoff, E.L. Synanon in drug addiction. In *Handbook of psychiatric therapies,* ed. J.H. Masserman. New York: Science House, 1966.

Marino, V.C. *The Habilitat, Inc.* Hawaii: Kaneohe Aloha United Way, 1976.

Martin, R.L., C.R. Cloninger, and S.B. Guze. Alcoholism and female criminality. *Journal of Clinical Psychiatry* **43**, no. 10 (1982): 400–403.

Marvit, R.C. Improving behavior of delinquent adolescents through group therapy. *Hospital and Community Psychiatry* **23** (1972): 239–242.

Maskin, M.B. The differential impact of work-oriented vs. communication-oriented juvenile correction programs upon recidivism rates in delinquent males. *Journal of Clinical Psychology* **32** (1976): 432–433.

________, and E. Brookins. The effects of parental composition on recidivism rates in delinquent girls. *Journal of Clinical Psychology* **30** (1974): 341–342.

Meichenbaum, D.H., K.S. Bowers, and R.R. Ross. Modification of classroom behavior of institutionalized female adolescent offenders. *Behavior Research and Therapy* **6** (1968): 343–353.

Meler, R.D., J. Crotty, and J. Dougherty. *Merger of research, training and treatment and a sample of research with women offenders.* Tallahassee, Florida: Florida State University School of Criminology, 1979.

Meyer, H.J., E.F. Borgatta, and W.C. Jones. *Girls at vocational high school.* New York: Russell Sage Foundation, 1965.

Miller, E.E. The woman offender and community corrections. In *Corrections in the community*, by E.E. Miller and M.R. Montilla. Reston, Va.: Reston Publishing Co., 1977.

________, and M. R. Montilla. *Corrections in the community.* Reston, Va.: Reston Publishing Co., 1977.

Miller, J.S., J. Sevsig, R. Stocker, and R. Campbell. Value patterns of drug addicts as a function of race and sex. *International Journal of the Addictions* **8**, no. 4 (1973): 589–598.

Milton, C.H., C. Pierce, M. Lyons, and C. A. Furry. *Female offenders, problems and programs.* Washington, D.C.: American Bar Association, 1976.

________, ________, ________, and B. Hippensteel. *Little sisters and the law.* Washington, D.C.: American Bar Association, 1977.

Minnesota Governor's Commission on Crime Prevention and Control. *Minnesota group residence for girls: Evaluation.* 1973.

Molof, M.J. *Statistical prediction of recidivism among parolees in the California Youth Authority*. Sacramento: California Department of the Youth Authority, 1970.

Morton, J.B. Women offenders: Fiction and facts. *American Journal of Corrections* (November 1976): 32–34.

Muson, H. Moral thinking: Can it be taught? *Psychology Today* (February 1979): 48–92.

Nacci, P. *Sexual assault study*. Paper presented at the Bureau of Prisons Conference on the Confinement of Female Offenders. Lexington, Ky.: March 1978.

Neto, V.V. Expanding horizons – Work and training for female offenders. *Corrections Today* **43** (1981), 66–72.

News Notes *(Clearinghouse on offender literacy.)* Washington, D.C.: American Bar Association, Fall 1975.

Nicolai, S. The upward mobility of women in corrections. In *Prison guard/correctional officer,* ed. R.R. Ross. Toronto: Butterworth, 1981.

Norland, S., and P.J. Mann. Being troublesome: Women on probation. *The Prison Journal* **64**, no. 1 (1984).

North, D.S. Breaking the training mold. *Manpower* (February 7, 1975).

Ochroch, R. *An evaluation of comparative changes in personality in adolescent delinquent boys and girls in a residential treatment setting*. Ph.D. dissertation, New York University, 1957.

O'Donnell, C.R., T. Lydgate, and W.S. Fo. The buddy system: Review and follow-up. In *Effective correctional treatment,* ed. R.R. Ross and P. Gendreau. Toronto: Butterworth, 1980.

Ollendick, T.H., and M. Hersen. Social skills training for juvenile delinquents. *Behavior Research and Therapy* **17** (1979): 547–554.

Ostrom, T.M., C.M. Steele, C.T. Rosenblood, and H.L. Mirels. Modification of delinquent behavior. *Journal of Applied Psychology* **1**, no. 2 (1971): 118–136.

Palmer, T. *Correctional intervention and research*. Lexington, Mass.: D.C. Heath, 1978.

Palmer, T.B. *Synopsis of California's group home project final report*. Sacramento: California Department of the Youth Authority, 1972.

Pappenfort, D.M., and C. H. Shireman. *The proctor program, New Bedford, Massachusetts.* Draft paper, national study of juvenile detention, University of Chicago, 1976.

Pauze, V.K. *Parole prediction in Iowa.* Iowa Women's Reformatory, 1982.

Peirce, F. J. Social group work in a women's prison. *Federal Probation* **27** (1963): 37–43.

Pemberton, D.A. A comparison of the outcome of treatment in female and male alcoholics. *British Journal of Psychiatry* **113** (1967): 367–373.

Pennsylvania Program for Women and Girl Offenders. *Task Force report on the state correctional institution at Muncy, Pa.* Washington, D.C.: Female Offender Resource Center, 1970.

Phillips, E.L., E.E. Phillips, D. Fixsen, and M. Wolf. Behavior shaping works for delinquents. *Psychology Today* (June 1973): 75–79.

Pierce, C.R., R.F. Asarnow, and R.R. Ross. Patterns of female delinquency: Toward differential treatment of female offenders. *South African Journal of Criminal Law and Criminology* **2**, no. 1 (1978): 278–287.

Piercy, F, and R.M. Lee. Effects of a dual treatment approach on the rehabilitation of habitual juvenile delinquents. *Rehabilitation Counseling Bulletin* **19** (1976): 482–492.

Platt, J.J., C. Labate, and R.J. Wicks. *Evaluative research in correctional drug abuse treatment.* Lexington, Mass.: D.C. Heath, 1977.

Podolsky, E. The woman alcoholic and premenstrual tension. *Journal of the American Medical Women's Association* **18** (1963): 816–818.

Potter, J. In prison, women are different. *Corrections Magazine* (December 1978): 14–47.

________. Women's work? The assault on sex barriers in prison job training. *Corrections Magazine* **5** (1979): 43–46, 48–49.

Redfering, D.L. Durability of effects of group counseling with institutionalized delinquent females. *Journal of Abnormal Psychology* **82**, no. 1 (1973): 85–86.

________. Group counseling with institutionalized delinquent females. *American Corrections Journal* **26** (1972): 160–163.

Renner, W. *Sentencing and release practices, State Correctional Institute at Muncy Pa., 1957–58 and 1971–73.* Washington,D.C.: Female Offender Resource Center, 1975.

Resnick, J., and N. Shaw. Prisoners of their sex—health problems of incarcerated women. *Prisoners' Rights Newsletter* (1980).

Ris, H.W. The integration of a comprehensive medical program in juvenile correctional institution. *Journal of the American Medical Women's Association* **30** (1975): 367–378.

________, and R. W. Dodge. Gonorrhea in adolescent girls in a closed population. *American Journal of Diseases of Children* **123** (1972): 135–189.

________, and ________. Trichomoniasis and yeast vaginitis in institutionalized adolescent girls. *American Journal of Diseases of Children* **125** (1973): 206–209.

Robinson, J., and G. Smith. The effectiveness of correctional programs. *Crime and Delinquency* **17** (1971): 67–80.

Rogers, S., and C. Carey. *Child-care needs of female offenders.* Toronto: Ministry of Correctional Services, 1979.

Romig, D.A. *Justice for our children.* Lexington, Mass.: D.C. Heath, 1978.

Rosenthal, B.J., M.J. Savoy, B.T. Greene, and W.H. Spillane. Drug treatment outcomes: Is sex a factor? *The International Journal of the Addictions* **14**, no. 1 (1979): 45–62.

Ross, J., and E. Hefferman. Women in a coed joint. *Quarterly Journal of Corrections* **10** (1977): 24–28.

Ross, R.R. From therapy to teaching: Some reflections on effective correctional programming. *Canada's Mental Health* **30** (1982): 1–13.

________, C. Currie and B. Krug-McKay. *The female offender: Treatment and training.* Toronto: Ministry of Correctional Services, 1980.

________, and E.A. Fabiano. *The cognitive model of crime and delinquency prevention and rehabilitation: I. Assessment procedures.* Toronto: Ministry of Correctional Services, 1983.

________, and ________. *The cognitive model of crime and delinquency prevention and rehabilitation: II. Intervention techniques.* Toronto: Ministry of Correctional Services, 1983.

________, and ________. *Time to think—Cognition and crime: Link and remediation.* Ottawa: Ministry of the Solicitor General of Canada, 1981.

________, and ________. *Time to think: The cognitive model of delin-*

quency prevention and offender rehabilitation. Johnson City, Tenn.: Institute of Social Sciences and Arts, 1985.

________, and P. Gendreau. *Effective correctional treatment.* Toronto: Butterworth, 1980.

________, and L. Lightfoot. *Treatment of the alcohol abusing offender.* Springfield, Ill.: C.C. Thomas, 1985.

________, and H.B. McKay. Adolescent therapists. *Canada's Mental Health* **24** (1976): 15–17.

________, and ________. Behavioral approaches to treatment in corrections: Requiem for a panacea. *Canadian Journal of Criminology & Corrections* **20** (1978): 279–295.

________, and ________. *Self-mutilation.* Lexington, Mass.: D.C. Heath, 1979.

________, D.H. Meichenbaum, and G. Humphrey. Treatment of nocturnal headbanging by behavior modification techniques. *Behavior Research and Therapy* **9** (1971): 151–154.

________, and W.R.T. Palmer. Modification of emotional expressiveness in adolescent offenders. *Crime and Justice* **4**, nos. 2–3 (1976): 125–133.

Rothenberg, E. *Effects of self-disclosure on social adjustment of institutionalized delinquent girls.* Ph.D. dissertation, University of New Mexico, 1969.

Roundtree, G.A., and A. Faily. The impact of educational programs on acts of aggression and rule violations in a female prison population. *Corrective and Social Psychiatry and Journal of Behavior Technology, Methods and Therapy* **26**, no. 3 (1980): 144–145.

Ruback, Barry. The sexually integrated prison: A legal and policy evaluation. *American Journal of Criminal Law* (Winter 1975): 301–330.

Sacks, B.K. Case for coeducational institutions. *Offender Rehabilitation* **2**, no. 3 (1978): 255–259.

San Diego County Probation Department. *Research and evaluation of the first year of operations of the San Diego County Juvenile Narcotics Project.* San Diego: 1971.

Sanson-Fisher, R.W., F.W. Seymour, and D. M. Baer. Training institutional staff to alter delinquents' conversation. *Journal of Behavior Therapy and Experimental Psychiatry* **7** (1976): 243–247.

________, ________, W. Montgomery, T. Stokes. Modifying delinquents' conversation using token reinforcement of self-recorded behavior. *Journal of Behavior Therapy and Experimental Psychiatry* **9** (1978): 163–168.

Sarason, I.G. A cognitive social learning approach to juvenile delinquency. In *Psychopathic behavior: Approaches to research*, ed. R.D. Hare and D. Schalling. New York: Wiley, 1978.

________. Verbal learning, modelling and juvenile delinquency. *American Psychologist* **23**, no. 4 (1968): 254–266.

Scharf, P., and J. Hickey. The prison and the inmate's conception of legal justice: An experiment in democratic education. *Criminal Justice and Behavior* **3** (1976): 107–122.

Schlossman, S., and S. Wallach. Crime of precocious sexuality—female juvenile delinquency in the progressive era. *Harvard Educational Review* **48**, no. 1 (1978): 65–74.

Schoonmaker, M.H., and J.S. Brooks. Women in probation and parole. *Crime and Delinquency* **21**, no. 2 (1975): 109–115.

Schuckit, M.A. and E.R. Morrissey. Alcoholism in women: Some clinical and social perspectives with an emphasis on possible subtypes. In *Alcoholism problems in women and children,* ed. M. Greenblatt and M.A. Schuckit. New York: Grune & Stratton, 1976.

Schultz, A.M. *Radical feminism: A treatment modality for addicted women.* Paper presented at the National Drug Abuse Conference Panel on Special Concerns of Women, Chicago, March 30–April 1, 1974.

Schweber, C. Beauty marks and blemishes: The coed prison as a microcosm of integrated society. *The Prison Journal* **64**, no. 1 (1984).

________. *The education of women prisoners: The Alderson legacy revisited.* Testimony before the House Committee on the Judiciary, Washington, D.C., October 11, 1979.

Scott, D., and H.L. Goldberg. The phenomenon of self-perpetuation in Synanon-type drug treatment programs. *Hospital and Community Psychiatry* **24** (1973): 231–233.

Scutt, J.A. Toward the liberation of the female offender. *International Journal of Criminology and Penology* **6** (1978): 5–18.

Seymour, F.W., and R. W. Sanson-Fisher. Effects of teacher attention on the classroom behavior of two delinquent girls within a token programme. *New Zealand Journal of Educational Studies* **10**, no. 2 (1975): 111–120.

———, and T.F. Stokes. Self-recording in training girls to increase work and evoke staff praise, in an institution for offenders. *Journal of Applied Behavior Analysis* **9** (1976): 41–54.

Simon, R.J. *Women and crime*. Lexington, Mass.: D.C. Heath, 1975.

Singer, L.R. Women and the correctional process. *American Criminal Law Review* **11** (1973): 300–308.

Skoler, D.L., and J.C. McKeown. *Women in detention and statewide jail standards.* Washington, D.C.: American Bar Association, 1974.

Slack, C. W., and E. N. Slack. It takes three to break a habit. *Psychology Today* (February 1976): 48–50.

Smart, C. *Women, crime and criminology*. London: Routledge & Kegan Paul, 1976.

Smykla, B. *Co-ed prisons.* New York: Human Sciences Press, 1980.

Sobel, S.E. Women in prison—sexism behind bars. *Professional Psychology* (April 1980): 331–338.

Sobell, M.B. and L.C. Sobell. Second year treatment outcome of alchoholics treated by individualized behavior therapy: Results. *Behavior Research and Therapy* **14** (1976): 195–215.

Sojourn, Inc. *Independent living program.* Described in Milton et al., 1977, p. 44.

Sowles, R.C., and J.H. Gill. Institutional and community adjustment of delinquents following counseling. *Journal of Consulting and Clinical Psychology* **34** (1970): 398–402.

Spence, S., and G. Shepheard. *Developments in social skills training*. New York: Academic Press, 1983.

Spencer, C., and J. E. Berecochea. *Vocational training at the California Institution for Women: An evaluation.* California Department of Corrections Report #4, 1972.

Stanton, A. M. *When mothers go to jail.* Lexington, Mass.: Lexington Books, 1980.

Suarez, J.M., V.G. Haddox, and H. Mittman. The establishment of a therapeutic community within a women's correctional facility. *Journal of Forensic Science* **17** (1972): 561–567.

Switzer, A. *Drug abuse and drug treatment.* Sacramento: California Department of the Youth Authority, 1974.

Sykes, R.A., and P.E. Green. Delinquent girls. *Vital Issues* **27**, no. 9 (1978): 1-6.

Tamerin, J.S., A. Tolor, and B. Harrington. Sex differences in alcoholics: A comparison of male and female alcoholics' self and spouse perceptions. *American Journal of Drug and Alcohol Abuse* **3**, no. 3 (1976): 457-472.

Taylor, A.J.W. An evaluation of group psychotherapy in a girl's borstal. *International Journal of Group Psychotherapy* **17**, no. 2 (1967): 168-177.

Taylor, J.L., J.L. Singer, H. Goldstein, and M. D. Tsaltas. *Group home for adolescent girls: Practice and research.* New York: Child Welfare League of America, 1976.

Tharp, R., and R. Wetzell. *Behavior modification in the natural environment.* New York: Academic Press, 1969.

Thelen, M.H., and J.L. Fryrear. Imitation of self-reward standards by black and white female delinquents. *Psychological Reports* **29** (1971): 667-671.

Thomas, R.G. De-institutionalization—managing independent living—an adult education prognosis for incarcerated women. *Journal of Correctional Education* **32** (1981): 11-14.

Thompson, G. R. Institutional programs for female offenders. *Canadian Journal of Corrections* **10**, no. 2 (1968): 438-44.

Truax, C.B., D.G. Wargo, and L.D. Silber. Effects of group psychotherapy with high accurate empathy and nonpossessive warmth upon female institutionalized delinquents. *Journal of Abnormal Psychology* **71**, no. 4 (1966): 267-274.

________, ________, and N.R. Volksdorf. Antecedents to outcome in group counseling with institutionalized juvenile delinquents. *Journal of Abnormal Psychology* **76**, no. 2 (1970): 235-242.

Turner, E. *Girls' group home: An approach to treating delinquent girls in the community.* Community treatment project report series, No. 1. Sacramento: California Department of the Youth Authority, 1969.

Upshur, C.C. *Field City Girls Center—A community-based program for delinquent girls.* Ph.D. dissertation, Harvard University, 1975.

Uzoka, A.F. The myth of the nuclear family. *American Psychologist* **34** (1979): 1095-1106.

Varki, C.P. *Sleighton School project change through group processes: Evaluation report.* Pennsylvania Governor's Justice Commission, 1977.

Velimesis, M.L. The female offender. *Crime and Delinquency Literature* **7**, no. 1 (1975): 94–112.

________. Sex roles and mental health of women in prison. *Professional Psychology* **12**, no. 1 (1981) 128–135.

Venezia, P. Unofficial probation: An evaluation of its effectiveness. *The Journal of Research in Crime and Delinquency* **9** (1972): 149–170.

Voegtlin, W.L., and W.R. Broz. The conditioned reflex treatment of chronic alcoholism: X. An analysis of 3125 admissions over a period of ten and a half years. *Annals of Internal Medicine* **30** (1949): 580–597.

Von Hilsheimer, G., W. Philpott, W. Buckley, and S.D. Klotz. Correcting the incorrigible: A report of 229 incorrigible adolescents. *American Laboratory* **101** (1977): 107–118.

Wade, T.C., T. Morton, J. Lind, and N. Ferris. A family crisis intervention approach to diversion from the juvenile justice system. *Juvenile Justice* **28**, no. 3 (1977): 43–51.

Wadsworth, M. *Roots of delinquency: Infancy, adolescence and crime.* Oxford: Robertson, 1979.

Wagner, B.R., and R.G. Breitmeyer. Pace: A residential, community oriented behavior modification program for adolescents. *Adolescence* **10**, no. 38 (1975): 277–286.

Wallgren, H., and H. Barry. *Actions of alcohol,* Vol. II. Amsterdam: Elsevier, 1970.

Walter, T.L., and C. M. Mills. A behavioral employment intervention program for reducing juvenile delinquency. In *Effective correctional treatment,* ed. R.R. Ross and P. Gendreau. Toronto: Butterworth, 1980.

Warren, M.Q. The female offender. In *Psychology of crime and criminal justice,* ed. H. Toch. New York: Holt, Rinehart & Winston, 1979.

Wayson, B.L. *Community programs for women offenders: Cost and economic considerations.* Washington, D.C.: American Bar Association, 1975.

Weathers, L., and R.P. Liberman. Contingency contracting with families of delinquent adolescents. *Behavior Therapy* **6** (1975): 352–366.

Weir, A. When the key turns. *Spare Rib* (May 1973): 26–27.

Weis, J.G. Liberation and crime. *Crime and Social Justice* (Fall 1976): 17–27.

Weitzel, S.L., and W. R. Blount. Incarcerated female felons and substance abuse. *Journal of Drug Issues* **12**, no. 3 (1982): 259–273.

Wheeler, M.E. The current status of women in prisons. In *The female offender,* ed. A.M. Brodsky. London: Sage Public, 1975.

________. Health care and needs of women. Proceedings of the second National Conference on Medical Care and Health Services in Correctional Institutions, 1978.

Widom, C.S. An empirical classification of female offenders. *Criminal Justice and Behavior* **6** (1978): 365–382.

Wiepert, G.D., P.T. d'Orban, and T.H. Bewley. Delinquency by opiate addicts treated at two London clinics. *British Journal of Psychiatry* **134** (1979): 14–23.

Williams, K. Health care for women inmates at the New Mexico State Penitentiary. Proceedings of the second National Conference on Medical Care and Health Services in Correctional Institutions, 1978.

Wilsnack, S.C. The impact of sex roles and women's alcohol use and abuse. In *Alcoholism problems in women and children*, ed. M. Greenblatt and M.A. Schuckit. New York: Grune & Stratton, 1976.

________. The needs of the female drinker: Dependency, power, or what? Proceedings of the Second Annual Alcoholism Conference of the National Institute on Alcohol Abuse and Alcoholism, 1973.

________. Sex role identity in female alcoholism. *Journal of Abnormal Psychology* **82** (1973): 253–261.

Wilson, H. Parental supervision: A neglected aspect of delinquency. *British Journal of Criminology* **20** (1980): 203–235.

Index

A

B

E

F

G

H

I

J

K

L

M

N

O

P

R

S

T

U

V

W

Y